Rhythmic Echoes and Reflections

KATHAK

Rhythmic Echoes and Reflections provides a glimpse into the little known facts connected with Kathak, the classical dance form of the Indo-Gangetic belt. While encompassing a detailed essay on the historical development of the dance form and its technical aspects, it is also a fascinating study on the continuity of the form and stance employed in the dance through a careful study of sculptures and paintings of the area beginning from the Mauryan period. It is a study of the 'devadasi' system in the region, the origin of the terms employed and their relation to the prevailing social conditions of the era and the philosophical attitudes underlying them—all of which are mirrored in the repertoire of Kathak.

———— • ————

Shovana Narayan is a Kathak dance virtuoso who has enthralled audiences at home and abroad with her scintillating recitals. While being strongly grounded in the centuries-old tradition of Kathak, she has successfully added new dimensions to it through innovative use of contemporary themes and poetry. With her fresh approach, creativity, sensitivity and innovation, she has broken new ground and proved herself to be a pioneer by enacting several scripts on the lives of sages and on issues of social concern. In recognition of her outstanding achievements, contributions and dedication to the arts, several awards have been showered on her, including the Padmashri by the Government of India, the Sahitya Kala Parishad Award, the Bihar State Award and the Oisca Award (Japan).

———— • ————

RHYTHMIC ECHOES AND REFLECTIONS: KATHAK
Shovana Narayan

OTHER LOTUS TITLES

IRADJ AMINI	*Koh-i-noor*
RUSKIN BOND	*Ruskin Bond's Green Book*
LALI CHATTERJEE	*Muonic Rhapsody and Other Encounters*
GIRISH CHATURVEDI	*Tansen*
NINA EPTON	*Mumtaz Mahal: Beloved Empress*
NAMITA GOKHALE	*Mountain Echoes: Reminiscences of Kumaoni Women*
MUSHIRUL HASAN	*India Partitioned: The Other Face of Freedom*, 2 vols.
	Knowledge, Power & Politics: Educational Institutions in India
JYOTI JAFA	*Nurjahan*
ASHISH KHOKAR	*Baba Allauddin Khan*
P. LAL	*The Bhagavad Gita*
JOHN LALL	*Begum Samru*
MAGGI LIDCHI-GRASSI	*The Great Golden Legend of the Mahabharata*, 2 vols.
MANOHAR MALGONKAR	*Dropping Names*
V. S. NARAVANE	*Best Stories from the Indian Classics*
V. S. NARAVANE	*Devadas and Other Stories by Sarat Chandra*
A. S. PAINTAL	*Ustad Amir Khan*
L. K. PANDIT	*Krishna Rao Shankar Pandit*
E. JAIWANT PAUL	*'By My Sword and Shield'*
E. JAIWANT PAUL	*Rani of Jhansi: Lakshmi Bai*
AMRITA PRITAM	*The Other Dimension*
VIBHUTI NARAIN RAI	*Curfew in the City*
GANESH SAILI	*Glorious Garhwal*
ARJAN SINGH	*Arjan Singh's Tiger Book*
DHANANAJAYA SINGH	*The House of Marwar*
KHUSHWANT SINGH	*Kipling's India*
MANJARI SINHA	*Ustad Bade Ghulam Ali Khan*
J.C. WADHAWAN	*Manto Naama*

FORTHCOMING TITLES

K. M. GEORGE	*The Best of Thakazhi Sivasankara Pillai*
SUDHIR KAKAR	*Indian Love Stories*
C. M. NAIM	*Zikr-e-Mir*
AMRITA PRITAM	*Fire in the Mirror*
LAKSHMI SUBRAMANIAN	*Medieval Seafarers*

Rhythmic Echoes and Reflections

KATHAK

SHOVANA NARAYAN

LOTUS COLLECTION
ROLI BOOKS

Lotus Collection

This edition first published 1998
The Lotus Collection
An imprint of
Roli Books Pvt Ltd
M-75, G.K. II Market
New Delhi 110 048
Phones: 6442271, 6462782, 6460886
Fax: 6467185
Also at
Varanasi, Agra, Jaipur and the Netherlands

CL   8/00
793. 31954

ISBN: 81-7436-049-2

s ring dance. Kangra, 1815; 41.5 x 31 cms
C.L. Bharani Collection

Photo Credits: Alok Kumar Jain for 'The laughing nati' on page 30
and the dancer from Pataliputra on the left on page 31.
Ashwini Chopra for dancer executing a pirouette on page 30.

Typeset in Galliard by Roli Books Pvt Ltd and
printed at Pritha Offsets Pvt Ltd, New Delhi-110 028

Contents

KATHAK   7

CLASSICAL DANCE FORMS   43

KATHAK AND THE SHASTRAS   51

SYMBOLISM IN DANCE POETICS   83

DANCE AND MUSIC   97

COSTUMES AND INSTRUMENTS   111

PATRONAGE AND SCHOOLS   125

CHANGING AESTHETICS   137

EMOTIONS, GESTURES AND MOVEMENTS   147

SUMMARY   155

SELECT READINGS   164

APPENDIX   167

Kathak

————— ❀ —————

Dance and music have always played an important part in India's religions and social life. Its rich culture and religious and philosophical thoughts have evolved over 5000 years as a result of interculturalism of the pre-Aryan and Aryan practices and concepts. The beauty of creation inspired a sense of wonder and humility before this 'power'. Worship which grew out of this sure of awe utilised dance as its vehicle of expression. The various evidences available in the last 2500 years from the Indus-Gangetic region reveals the presence of dance in the region which was performed by both men and women. The stories of the bards from which epic compositions originated, lent themselves to dance and music presentations. These were the 'Kathaks' · or the 'kushilavs' of Valmiki's *Ramayana*, 'kauthumaris', 'nautankis', 'rasadharis' and 'swaangs' in the Gangetic belt. The Amarkosha refers to the 'kushilavs' as:

shailalinastu shailusha jayajeeva krishashwinah
bharat ityapi natashcharanastu kushilavah

(shailali, shailusha, jayajeeva, krishashvi, bharata, nata, charana and kushilav are the six names of 'natas').

In the *Kalpadruma*, the 'kushilava' has been described as those who practice the art of drama through story-telling:

kushilava vrityartha natyashastra pracharkatvat valmiki muniti

According to the *Natyashastra*, 'kushilava' are persons well-versed in music and dramatics and are able to utilise their creative faculties. 'Kushilavs', who are also known as 'charanas', are referred to in the *Sangeet Ratnakar* as those who narrate and have absolute knowledge of all the 'ragas', dance and ankle-bells, the latter being also used as musical instruments:

kinkinivadhvedi ca vriito vikatnartakaih
marmagyah sarvarageshu chaturashcharano matah

The 'Kathakas' of the *Mahabharata* were a special group of story-telling brahmins, establishing identifying ties with the Kathak tradition of our day. In a passage in the Arjunavanvasa section of the Adiparva in the *Mahabharata*, there is an indirect reference to the art practised by the Kathaks:

Kathakascapare rajan sramanasca vanaukasah
divyakhyanani ye capi pathanti madhuram dvijah

(Arjun, on his departure for the forest, was accompanied by an entourage of Kathaks and forest dwelling ascetics and brahmins who recited sweetly the divine tales).

Thus, the skill of the Kathaks in articulation was a professional characteristic and they, therefore, belonged to that class of men whose work was associated with oral meditations in the sacred traditions.

Indication that the Kathaks were brahmins are given in the Anusasnika-parva of the *Mahabharata*, in an enumeration of the various kinds of brahmins who ranked above those brahmins conducting the 'sraddhas' (ceremony following death):

*gayana nartakascai' va plavaka vadakastakha
Kathaka yodhakscai' va rajan na rhanti ketanam*

(singers, dancers, rope dancers, instrumentalists, Kathaks and fighters are not to be invited, O'king).

These references indicate the existence of dancing story-tellers in the pre-Christian era. Thus, it appears that Kathak, as the name suggests, originated in the Indus-Gangetic belt where the brahmins (priests) while recounting stories based on Hindu mythology reached the point of ecstasy in their devotion which manifested itself through the medium of dance. This dance form danced by the Kathakas or Kathaks in the ecstasy of their devotion was called Kathak derived from the words 'Kathakar' (story-teller) and 'katha' (story).

The *Kathasaritasagar* (11th century AD) records King Sahasratika listening to a Kathaka, Sangataka. Kaiyata (10th century AD) has equated the 'Kathaka' and the 'granthika' in his commentary Bhashyapradiga as both classes being synonymous in their professions. Sharangadeva's Sangeet Ratnakar (13th century AD) mentions the existence of 'kauthumari' i.e. singing accompanied by acting in the Samaveda as practised by the 'kauthums' and Guru Tumbaru.

In the 7th chapter of the *Sangeet Ratnakar*, mention has been made of the Kathaks which is as follows:

Kathaka bandinaschatra vidyavantah priyamvadah prashansakulashchanye chaturah sarvamatushu

(the Kathakas, the devotees, the enlightened etc. who recite sweetly, win the hearts of . . . . .)

According to *Abhidan Rajendra*, the Jain lexicon, 'kathya' means a type of music composition and 'kahaga' and 'kahub' as one who narrates the story in a vivid manner, find mention in the Kalpasutra and other Jain works. According to various Jain munis, the 'dharma' (profession) of the Kathak is to enact the stories through dance as expressed in the following shloka: *katha akoorti nibah:*

While 'kathiko' means a preacher in the Pali dictionary and an 'actor' in the Nepali dictionary, Kathak denotes a story-teller in the Sanskrit dictionary. The Kathak is a person who preaches the stories through the medium of acting: *kathayati yah sah Kathakah.*

There is also a reference to the 'Sumati Kathaks' in the *Ragatarangini* of Lochan (17th century) who were those brahmins who enacted out stories from the *Puranas* to Raja Sumati. In the *Ain-e-Akbari*, Abul Fazal has mentioned two distinct categories of male dancers, namely the professional dancers called 'natas' or 'natwas' and the 'brahmin' dancers called 'kirtaniyas' or 'Kathakiyas'.

William Crooke's census figures of 1891 indicate the presence of 569 Kathaks in Gorakhpur, 215 Kathaks in Azamgarh, 210 Kathaks in Rai Bareli and 149 Kathaks in Partapgarh. Similarly, the census conducted by James Prinsep in 1825 and Buchanan in 1814 in the regions of Benaras and Bihar respectively indicate the existence of more than hundred and fifty eight Kathak families together.

Simultaneously, the 'ras-leela' tradition of the 'rasdharis' of Brindaban and the 'bhaktiyas', the 'nrityakalis' and the 'jhumariyas' of various regions of Bihar and Eastern Uttar Pradesh, which had their birth during the Bhakti Movement (religious renaissance) sometime in the 14th and 15th centuries, are based on the Katha tradition.

A close interaction of religion with dance interwoven with the powerful impulse for expression became a way of life in Vedic India. Chanting of the Riga-vedic hymns was accompanied by ritual dancing. From a review of the music and dance scenario of the region, it emerges that:

a)   Dance was associated with rituals.

b)   Both men and women danced.

c)   Study of music and dance was part of the education process of royal princes and princesses.

d)   There existed many categories of dancers: the common people as well as the highly skilled professional groups.

e)   Amongst the professional groups, there were the exalted courtesan dancers and the temple dancers (the demarcation between the two was often blurred) as well as groups of male dancing priests.

f)   There existed some difference between the 'margi' and the 'desi' namely the classical and folk approaches, thus supporting the existence of highly trained professional groups of dancers together with dance as part of community activity.

g)   The references to 'apsaras' and 'yakshinis' as celestial dancers or water nymphs were allegories for extremely skilled and beautiful dancers.

h)   The style of dance danced in the temples or the courts was essentially the same.

In the Vedic age, prevalence of music and dance in society can be gleaned from various shlokas. The *Rigaveda* has

likened dance to nectar while the Prithvisookt in the
Atharvaveda describe the singing and dancing people on
earth as *yasyam gayanti nrityanti bhumyanmartyah.*
In the following verse of the *Samaveda*, the importance
of 'gandharva veda' relating to music and dance can be
seen:

vachamashtapdeemaham
navastraktimritavridhamindrat
paritanvam mame

(I receive from God, the knowledge of the vast, eight
footed Vedic speech consisting of the riga -*yajur-sama-
atharva*- vedas and the four upavedas namely ajurveda
(medicine), dhanurveda (military science), gandharva veda
(music and dance) and arthaveda (political science)).

Samagana was a very special feature of Vedic times. In
the tenth adhyaya of the *Bhagwada Gita*, Lord Krishna
declares, 'I am Samaveda among the Vedas'. Next to the
Vedas are the two great epics, the *Ramayana* and the
Mahabharata. The existence of dancers are evident at the
time of Lord Rama's coronation at Ayodhya.

natnartaka sanghanam gayakam ca' gayatam
yatahkarnasukhavachah sushrava janta tatah

(the people are entranced by hearing the sweet words in
the dance of the dancers and the songs of the singers).

The Ayodhyakand of *Ramayana* reveals that Lord Rama,
as a young prince, was trained in the 'gandharva veda' and
was, therefore, adept in the art of music and dance. He has
often been referred to as the 'gandharvaraja'. In the
Mahabharata, Arjun is supposed to have been an

accomplished dancer having learnt the art from 'gandharva' Chitrasena:

geetamvaditram nrityani bhooya evadideshah
tathapi talamachharma tarasvi drutkaritam
sa shikshito nrityagunananekan vaditra
geetartha gunascha sarvan
na sharmalebhe parveerhanta bhratrina
smaranmatarshchaiva kuntim

(Well-versed in the arts of music and dance, Arjun, the victor over ruthless enemies, obeyed the advice of Kunti).

Furthermore, during his period of incognito exile, Arjun, as the eunuch Brihanalla, taught the art of dance to Uttara, daughter of King Virat of Matsya, the area between Alwar and Jaipur.

The Puranic period (4th century to 8th century AD approximately) saw many references to dance and dancers. According to the *Vishnupuran*, the mother of Vishal of the Ikshvaku dynasty at Vaishali, was an 'apsara' by the name of Alambusha, proficient in the arts of music and dance. The various Upanishads also refer to the existence of music and dance. In the *Vrihadaranyakopnishad*, there is a reference to Rishi Yagyavalkya who lived during the time of Raja Janak at Mithila and who believed that the practice of the fine arts were paths to 'moksha' (salvation).

Many references to dancers have been made in various Buddhist and Jain canons.

The sixth century BC in India saw the emergence of two new faiths: Jainism and Buddhism. During the pre-Mauryan, Mauryan and post-Mauryan periods, a prolific system of music and dance flourished as is evident from eminent dancers such as Amrapali, Salvati, Padmavati, Roopkosha, Upkosha, etc. Similarly, the curriculum at

Nalanda University had music and dance as its subjects.

The importance of the involvement of artistes and dancers in the state administration has been dwelt upon by Chanakya (or Kautilya), prime minister during the reign of Chandragupta Maurya, in his Arthashastra (a treatise on state administration). There was a flowering of art and architecture, the use of script and the system of 'shrenis' (guilds), the latter giving rise to hereditary professions. Music and dance became an integral part of each household. Specialised knowledge began to be handed down from father to son even while disseminating the art amongst the common people. There was a clear distinction between the trained dancers and the common dancers. Differences between skilled and trained dancers and popular dancers have been given in the *Arthashastra* and also in the *Samaveda*. Difference between 'ganikas' (courtesans) and the trained courtesan dancers and the 'nartakas' (dancers) have been highlighted in the 'rasyaranga' episode of the *Ramayana* where the categories of the 'natas', 'nartakas' and 'ganikas' are mentioned distinctly and also the fact that no festivity or ceremonial occasions could take place without them. The 'apsaras' were also taken tobe excellent courtesan dancers. In a few references, the 'ganikas' seem to refer to those courtesans whose main forte lay in singing and music. There was also the distinct group of the 'kushilavs' and the 'Kathakas' associated with the art of story-telling. The dance teachers have been referred to as the 'sailusa' in the *Ayodhyakand* of Valmiki's *Ramayana* as well as in the *Yajurveda* and bears a close relation to the 'silalin' of Panini and Bharata's *Natyashastra* and the 'sailali' of the *Harshacharita*. Kautilya has differentiated between the 'nartaka' and the 'kusilava'. While the former was a trained dancer, the latter was a story-teller through dance. He also maintains a difference between a temple-associated dancer and a classical dancer but these fine distinctions overlap in other subsequent works.

Mention has been made about the movement of professional groups of artistes from one place to another involving a maximum stay of 15 days during the monsoons. The *Arthashastra* also refers to the members of the royal household being trained in the fine arts. As Patliputra was the capital and, therefore, the political centre during the Mauryan times, the experience of Megasthenes, the Greek ambassador to the court of Chandragupta Maurya is significant. In his *Indica*, he dwells on dances for rituals and comments on the dance halls attached to temples and palaces. Various Buddhist stories and the Vinay texts reveal the presence of many courtesan dancers such as Amrapali (or Ambapali), Salvati, Padmavati and Vimla. It emerges that the pre-Mauryan and Mauryan period saw the 'nagar badhu' (state dancer) system at Vaishali and Patliputra, implying the high standards of perfection attained in dance along with the power and prestige supposedly enjoyed by them. Many Jain texts such as the *Brihatkalpa*, *Srikalpasutra*, *Vayadhammakaha*, mention.

In the *Uttarapithika*, Ragamanjari is a woman described with rare artistic endowment whose dances in the 'pancavira goshthi' have been praised. Similarly, like the 'samajjas' of the Lichhavis, the 'nrityagoshthis' have been mentioned in the *Harshacharita* along with 'sailali', 'nartaki' and the 'lasaka' categories of dancers. Dances such as the 'hallisaka', 'charchari' or 'natyarasaka' and 'rasa' find mention in Bhasa's *Balcharita*, Harsha's *Ratnavali* and the *Bhagwadpurana* respectively.

Panikkar writes 'among the 64 arts which a well-educated man was supposed to know, dancing and music ranked high'. Vatsyayan, while describing the life of a citizen mentions the keeping of musical instruments thereby indicating 'the interest of every household in fine arts'.

Patliputra continued to be the centre of political power even during the Gupta period which saw the golden age of classicism in ancient India. This period saw the flowering literary, cultural, social and political activities and also saw both the Mahayana and Hinayana forms of Buddhism flourishing throughout the empire. At the same time, Hinduism was revived and reached its golden age.

Many compilations of literary works were done during this period. Most of the Gupta rulers were proficient in the fine arts of music and dance, with Samudragupta being the outstanding artiste amongst members of this royal dynasty. He himself was an accomplished 'veena' player (displayed on the coins of his period), and also patronised writers and artistes. The *Kathasaritasagar* refers to Patliputra (present day Patna in Bihar) as an abode of culture, learning and fine arts. The written accounts of various Chinese travellers such as Fahien (in 399-411 AD during the reign of Vikramaditya), Hiuen-tsang (around 606 AD during the reign of Harshavardhana) and Itsing, refer to the prevalence of music and dance in daily life. Fahien describes the *rathyatras* (chariot festivals) taken out at Patliputra every year on the 8th day of the second month preceded by a galaxy of musicians and dancers.

Efflorescence and fulfillment of the gradual development in the field of arts were achieved to a degree of perfection never achieved before in the realms of music, dance, literature, drama, sculpture, architecture and the plastic arts. Decorations on pillars and friezes while giving an extremely rich and baroque effect have provided an insight into the form of dance prevalent then. Of the few surviving gems of the Gupta period, the reliefs and figures in the temples at Deogarh reveal, the 'sense of emergence from the limitless background; their faces reveal a rapt, entranced expression of absorption in their own being; and the forms move in each curvilinear rhythm, their contours intermingling with the fluidity of waves or flames.' Sanskrit was the language of the educated upper caste while Pali and Prakrit, the popular forms of Sanskrit, were spoken in towns and villages. This too, had its local variations: Shauraseni in the west and Magadhi in the east. Thus the usage of local languages and dialects such as Brajbhasha, Avadhi, Bhojpuri and Rajasthani in Kathak today is a logical development.

By the 10th century, signs of decay had become visible. Toynbee believes there was a weakening of the 'ancient spirit and characteristic soul'. Nonetheless, works of Raja Nanyadeva of the 10th -11th century of the Karnat dynasty at Mithila point to the continuing practice of music and dance in certain pockets of the Gangetic belt. The treatise, *Saraswati Hridayalankar* popularly known as *Bharatbhashya* and authored by Nanyadeva throws light on the various ragas in usage and its effect on the delineation of expression.

The establishment of Muslim rule in India witnessed a religious renaissance: the Bhakti Movement. With the rise of Vaishnavism as a consequence of the Bhakti Movement, the Gangetic belt witnessed a spurt in literature, poetry and dance. As mentioned in the book *Rasasarvaswa* in the 15th century, Swami Haridas encouraged Vithalnath, son of Vallabhacharya, to stage the rasa, a dance sequence woven around Lord Krishna. Ghamand Deva and later Narayan Bhatt revived the *ras-leela* in the area. Shri Vallabha, a Kathak from Rajasthan, was invited to Karhela near Vrindaban, in order to help stage the leela. Thus, the staging of the *ras-leela* gained ground with young boys, enacting the roles of Lord Krishna, Radha and the gopis (cow-maidens). The themes based on verses of poets including the *ashtachhap* poets from the Bhakti Movement namely, Haridas, Namdev, Surdas, Nand Das, Parmanand, Kumbhadas, Krishnadas, Chaturbhujdas, Govindaswami and Chittaswami were sung in the Dhrupad style and enacted out with mime and dance involving simple *toras-tukras* or rhythmic patterns in a simplistic Kathak style.

The *leela* shows begin with the traditional 'manglacharan' (an obeisance to the lord) followed by 'arti' (circling lights before an image), 'gopi prarthana' (prayer of the maidens), 'Radha prarthana' (prayer of Radha), 'rasa' (dance of Lord Krishna), 'leela' (sportive play) and 'pravachan' (exposition). At this point of time, the mobility of the Kathaks of western parts of India led them to newer pastures west of the Hindukush mountains. These Kathaks later retained the characteristic flavour of footwork, body language and some of the hand gestures but imbibed many Arabic and Judaic nuances during their travels resulting in the flamenco dance form of the Andalusian region of Spain.

In another stream of development, a small group of Kathaks especially in the regions of Rajasthan, Gujarat and western Madhya Pradesh introduced the 'kala-baazi': sensational aspects within the dance form such as dancing on the edge of a brass-plate, on a bed of 'gulal' (red powder), on beds of nails, swords and 'batasha' (sugar puffs) in a bid to please the local chieftains and rulers. As of today, there are very few surviving performers who stress these sensational aspects. However, the 'bhavai nritya' of western India has kept the tradition alive. Abul Fazal in his *Ain-e-Akbari*, has mentioned the dances of the 'bhanvayya' (or 'bhavaiya') who danced on 'thalis' (brass plates).

With the establishment of Muslim rule, rigid imposition of the 'purdah' (veil) and early marriages affected the practice of the arts. The emphasis was on architecture, music and painting by the early Mughals while some of the later Mughals indulged in entertainment and gave patronage to musicians and dancers. Some of the Persian dances of the medieval period such as those of the 'hournis' (or 'hourkinis'), 'domnis' and 'lolonis' which were on simplistic lines, were integrated into the fabric of Indian society. As with the case of 'apsara' of the Hindu mythology, a beautiful dancer is referred to as an 'apsara' or 'hourni' in various myths.

But the approach to music and dance as religious offerings practised by the Hindus was not in conformity with the principles of Islam and, therefore, it was not surprising to see localisation of the dance form. Some patronage was given to Kathak and the associated groups of dancers during the reign of Emperor Akbar owing to the influence of his Rajput Hindu wife, Jodhabai. However, the fullest expression of patronage came later with Nawab Wajid Ali Shah of Oudh (or Awadh) who was not only an accomplished poet but also a student of Kathak.

In pockets where Hindu rulers reigned, there still continued the tradition of patronage to music and dance as is evident from various works such as the *Sri Hastamuktavali* (a treatise on hand gestures as utilised in dance) by Shubhankar of Mithila and *Sangeet Damodar* (treatise on music), the *Varnaratnakar* (a treatise on music and dance) by Jyotishwar Thakur and the *Ragatarangini* by Lochan.

The *Ain-e-Akbari* of Abul Fazl also details the classification of dancers, instruments, music, themes and treatment within music and dance. A contemporary of Vallabhacharya, Guru Nanak (1469-1538) in his hymn Asa ki Var mentions actors and dancers in costumes enacting Krishna tales during his time. The hand-written manuscripts of Roop Goswamiji, disciple of Chaitanya Mahaprabhu and founder of the Govind Dev temple of *Gaudiya sampradaya* at Vrindaban and Shri Hitaharivansha Goswami, a contemporary of Swami Haridas, also bear witness to the widespread practice of dance in the sixteenth century, based on the legends of Lord Krishna.

Apart from dancing mystics and story-tellers, there were communities among whom dancing was a profession. Some of these were the 'dadhis', 'natwas', 'bhagtiyas', 'murakiyas', 'bhavaiya' or 'bhanvaiya', 'rasadharis', 'kanchanis', 'kirtaniyas' and 'Kathakas'. These dance forms flourished under the impetus and resurgence of Vaishnavism (i.e. based on the theme of Lord Krishna and Radha) and were pure Kathak in style, technique and form.

These works would not have been possible in the 15th to the 17th centuries had there not been a living atmosphere conducive to music and dance in the region. Whatever little patronage was given to the Kathak community of Churu-Sujangarh near Shekhawati and the dancers of the Mithila region in the sixteenth century by the local kings and nobles, circumstances changed with the coming of Aurangzeb as the Mughal ruler.

In the process, the courtesans proved an invaluable link between the temple priests or gurus and the society at large, in the maintenance and development of the music and dance systems. Some of the famous courtesans, renowned for their skill in music and dance, from the region of Avadh included Zohrabai, Mushtaribai, Sukhbadan and Gulbadan, (both of Benaras), Janbaksha Bandawali, Adhvan Unnaonivasi, Bi Lutfan, Chandrabai Akbarabadwali and Jaddanbai. Furthermore, there were the courtesans of the 'parikhana' of Nawab Wajid Ali Shah who performed 'rahas', a dance-drama conceptualised by the Nawab on inspiration drawn from the 'ras-leela'. In Rajasthan, some elements of Muslim culture had come to stay. Notable was the 'purdah-system' taking the form of 'ghunghat' which is still strong in some pockets of society. In the royal household, this translated itself into the 'zenana' (the feminine) system. A class of courtesans, skilled in artistic qualities sported the title of 'rai' as they danced not only for the 'zenanas' but also for the king on social and religious occasions. Some of the eminent courtesan-dancers from this area were Kishorebeli, Anandrai, Gulabrai, Jonrai, Govindi, Uttamrai, Chandarai and Kishorerai. In Patna, the night 'mehfils' called 'khari mehfil' starting at 8 pm lasted till the early hours of the morning when 'raga bhairavi' was sung. These 'mehfils' boasted of exceptionally gifted dancers such as Mahtab, Choudhrain, Zohrabai, Allah Jilai, Badi Kaneez and Haider Jan Begum many of whom find mention in Buchanan's travelogues.

Besides, there were many male dancer-cum-teachers apart from the traditional Kathak gurus. Fazal Hussain Bhand, Amanullah Khan and Ataullah Khan were such gifted dancers at Patna and Muzaffarpur respectively. At Lucknow, Kalandar Baksha, Mohammad Hussain, Ghulam Abbas, Haider Ali, Kayam Khan and Kanhaiya in addition to Prakashji Mishra (of the legendary Lucknow 'gharana'), Lalluji, Mansingh, Ram Sahay (of Hadia), Beni Prasad and Parasadu of Benaras were some notable names. Of these, Kayam Khan and Kanhaiya were disciples of Wajid Ali Shah.

It was Bindadin's grandfather, Prakashji Mishra, a Kathak, who moved from Hariya in Allahabad district into the court of Nawab Asaf-ud-daulah, while his son, Thakur Prasad, became the guru and mentor of Nawab Wajid Ali Shah in the art of Kathak. Though the Nawab ruled from 1847 to 1856 yet he laid the foundation of patronisation of Kathak and formalisation and stylisation of the art. While excelling in the art of dance, the artistes were also required to be well versed in the arts of singing, poetry writing and playing percussion and musical instruments. Thus, the best Kathak artiste with all the above requisites and having over 100 disciples was honoured with the title of 'Maharaj'. In keeping with this practice, the Kathak favoured by the Nawab of Oudh (Awadh) was also bestowed the title of Maharaj i.e. King of kings (amongst the dancers), which has now become a family title and has been handed down from generation to generation. This was the period which gave recognition to individuals as skilled artistes.

However, a clear distinction is to be kept between the true Kathaks maintaining the traditional spirit of the dance and persons who have studied Kathak nuances for some time and then are able to incorporate certain aspects into their dance. Viewed strictly, the dancing girl of north India, the 'nautch' or 'nachaniya' or 'nachni' cannot be termed as Kathaks. They were the common 'bais'; but there were many categories of dancers such as the 'dharimirasins', 'nagarnts', 'rais' and the 'rumzanis' who were considered good trained artistes technically. Often their teacher was a Kathak who imparted to them some aspects of the dance. Falling within these categories would be the women dancers during the time of Muhammad Shah. Muhammad Shah was one of the later Mughal rulers who had been given the title of 'rangile' (the colourful one) due to his passionate interest in the fine arts. Perhaps, one tends to overlook the immense patronage given to artistes of high calibre by Muhammad Shah as it is usual to describe him as the 'rangila' in a derogatory manner. The well-known singers Adarang and Sadarang were gems of his court and these singers, were the best artistes of their time.

After the death of Muhammad Shah in 1748, quite a few of the artistes seem to have migrated to various centres such as Lucknow, Alwar, Jaipur, Jodhpur and Raigarh. Thus, new pockets of patronage sprang up. It also indicated great mobility in the Kathak caste as this group comprised of hereditary brahmin dancers and also those who had been admitted to the occupation. The patronage of arts by temple orders and local courts continued during the British rule in India.

Influence of Muslim Rule

Any dance form, if alive today and sharing a long traditional history, owes its present position to the inherent dynamism within the dance-form, capable of withstanding all forms of onslaught while continuously adapting and innovating in the wake of changed circumstances,—socially, artistically and politically—and so it is with Kathak. One of the predominant factors was the external change of environment which was not the usual change of dynasties ruling the region but along with it, a change in the religious belief of the rulers of medieval India. Thus, with Muslim rule, some changes were to be seen in the practice of Kathak. As idol-worship goes against the tenets of the Islamic faith, the traditional male brahmin Kathak performers resorted to a heavy display of rhythmic virtuosity. Thus, this period saw furtherance of rhythmic patterns, the practice of 'sawal-jawab' (question and answer) between the dancer and the percussionist as well as the 'jugalbandi' (friendly competition), between two artistes. It was during this period that many 'farmaishi bols' (special patterns) were created. These 'bols' (rhythmic patterns) included patterns based on observance of moods of nature, sounds of instruments and life and animation.

In the field of 'abhinaya' (mimetic exposition) the element of Sufi interpretations were incorporated in the delineation of expression whereby 'Mohan' (Lord Krishna) or 'sajan' or 'saiyan' or 'piya' (beloved) became synonymous with the 'paramatma' (the Supreme Lord). However, this internalised religious feeling was misutilised and misinterpreted by common practitioners and lowly courtesans who equated 'Mohan piya' with the benefactor in the mimetic delineations of 'thumri', thus giving the dance a different colour. But interestingly, the contents and themes danced by genuine Kathaks continued to be strongly based on Krishna and Radha or Shiva-Parvati. In fact, even the great patron, Nawab Wajid Ali Shah wrote 'thumris' (under the pen name 'Akhtar') alluding to Hari or Krishna.

Some of the rhythmic pieces such as the 'salami' (the Muslim way of greeting) and the 'amad' (the rhythmic entry piece) came into vogue. But the 'salami' was replaced by 'rangmach ki pooja' (obeisance to the theatre and place of dance) in addition to the traditional 'stuti' (prayer to the Lord) in the courts of the Hindu rulers of eastern Uttar Pradesh, Rajasthan and Madhya Pradesh. However, the 'salami' was discontinued in the last 80 years or so.

The medieval period also saw the usage of many new instruments which till then were not associated with Kathak such as the tabla, sitar, sarod, sarangi and harmonium. The 'pakhawaj' was replaced by the 'tabla' as the main percussion instrument while the 'sarangi' or the 'harmonium' came to stay as the main keeper of the rhythmic cycle or the 'lehera'. Musical compositions made heavy utilisation of sitar, sarod, harmonium, sarangi, etc.

The tradition of dancing in the temple precincts and open spaces may be seen from the fact that the 'kirtaniyas' of the temple of Nathdwara (Rajasthan) danced in praise of Lord Krishna in the inner court at Dol Tiwari. Similarly, the 'bhaktiyas', 'nrityakalis' and the 'kalavagntis' danced in praise of Shiva-Parvati and Radha-Krishna in various parts of eastern Uttar Pradesh and Bihar.

The 20th century saw the:

• re-emergence from obscurity or from the confines of temple and court scenarios
• acceptance of the dance form and their performers in society in full measure
• conscious effort by artiste, art historians, lovers of music and dance to trace the roots and stages of development with a sense of pride and awareness of the rich cultural heritage inherited by us
• further formalisation of dance repertoires and manner of presentation
• unconscious assimilation of the changing ethos of the 20th century in the repertoire and presentation of dance.

Only the intimate temple and 'samajjas' (gatherings) for dance performances of ancient India has given way to dancing in large and formal theatres or auditoria of today with their inherent demands on choreography, lighting and sound requirements.

The entry pieces of the Muslim and Hindu courts, the 'salami' and the 'rangmanch-ki-pooja' were dropped from modern-day renderings of Kathak. Similarly, most of the 'gats' (gaits) introduced by Nawab Wajid Ali Shah disappeared from the horizon with the exception of a few such as the 'rukhsar' and 'chhapka gats'. The 'abhinaya' (mimetic expression) is rendered in its correct perspective, thereby rectifying some of the aberrations of the last few centuries.

In terms of costume, the artiste today has a choice between the 'lehenga-choli', the 'churidar-angarkha' and the 'sari' or some of their modern variants. While violin is being increasingly used, yet there is a diminishing use of the 'sarangi'.

The literature of the past 2500 years (with the exception of the late 19th century onwards) do not reveal the names of any outstanding or well-known male Kathaks. Names of women dancers such as Amrapali, Salvati, Kosha and Kuvalya, do appear in the various Buddhist and Jain canons only, despite male dancers having had a hegemony in the temples and also in the courts as may be seen by the training in fine arts given to the male members of the royal households. One reason for non-appearance of names of male dancers could be attributed to the fact that Indian society is not individualistic, for no account mentions the contribution of individuals to their respective field of art (barring adulation of the king). Mention of a few women dancers in the Buddhist and Jain religions works are incidental and not primarily because of their achievements as artistes.

Kathak, even with a strong Hindu base is, perhaps, the most secular of all dance forms displaying a beautiful synthesis of all that is best in the two distinct cultures belonging to both periods of political rule and consequent social ethos of the Indo-Gangetic belt.

System of Devadasi

Even though traditional Kathaks were the bards and the story-telling priests of the temples while the courtesans of 2400 years ago such as Amrapali and Salvati were accomplished dancers, yet the system of 'devadasi' was not unknown in the Indo-Gangetic belt. When the system of Hindu temple building came into prominence, the various temple rituals connected with the need for serving God also began. This gave birth to the system of singing and dancing girls who had to bathe, rock to sleep and entertain the Gods. Kalidasa makes a reference to the 'devadasis' in the Mahakala temple of Ujjain at the time of 'sandhya pooja' (evening worship) in his *Meghdoot* while amongst the earlier literary works, only the *Arthashastra* of Kautilya seems to have made a reference to the 'devadasi'. Most of the earlier works mention the courtesan-dancers and the various categories of 'kushilavs' (story-tellers and dancers). It, therefore, follows that the system of 'devadasi' started out as a regalia connected with temple duties and was endorsed in the later day *Puranas*. The following 'shloka' (verse) in the *Srishtikhanda* of the *Padmapurana* went to the extent of recommending the purchase of beautiful girls for dedication to the temples in order to attain heaven:

krita devaye datavya dheerenaklishtakarmana
kalpakalam bhavetsvargo nripo vaso mahadhani

The *Bhavishyapurana* also echoes a similar (goes to the extent of recommending dedication of girls to the sun temple in order to win 'suryalok' by the kings as is evident from) thought in the following verse:

veshyamdabakam yastu dadyatsooryaya bhaktitah
sa gachchhetparamam sthanam yatra tishthati bhanuman

By the sixth or seventh century AD, the system was well-established. From a few 'shlokas' in the *Puranas*, it also appears that childless couples pledged their first-born to the temples, which also added to the number of 'devadasis'.

Hiuen Tsang makes a reference to the number of 'devadasis' (dancing girls) he saw attached to the Sun temple at Multan while the *Rajatarangini* of Kalhana also indicates to the prevalence of this custom in Kashmir from about the 7th century AD onwards. This system was also not unknown at the Vishwanath temple at Benaras as is evident from the reference in *Kuttinimatam*. The Jogimara caves at Ramgarh hills in Bihar supports an inscription describing the love between Devadinna, a sculptor and Satunuka, a 'devadasi'.

Even though the system of 'devadasi' seems to have died down in the Indo-Gangetic belt with the establishment of Muslim rule when temple building came to a halt by about the 10th. century, some of the chronicles pertaining to the Mughal period refer to the existence of 'devadasis' in the temples of the Indo-Gangetic belt. One 'parwana' dated 25 January, 1644 AD (15 zulqada 1053 AH) written by Azam Khan mentions the presence of 'nrit-kanyan' (women dancers) in the Govind Dev temple at Vrindaban.

The practice of dedicating the first-born daughter to Lord Khandoba who eventually takes up her profession as a 'lavani-dancer', is seen even today in Maharashtra. The 'lavani' dances are influenced by Kathak; therefore, it is not uncommon to find Kathak footwork and rhythmic patterns within their presentations. This practice is also evident in the 'vaghya-murli' dancers of the state whose foreheads are smeared with turmeric. As turmeric has a symbolic significance in the context if a Hindu girl's marriage, therefore the 'murlis', supposed to be the wives of Lord Khandoba, apply turmeric on the forehead, denoting the fact that though married (to God) yet they are untouched by males.

This system was evident in pockets of Rajasthan even as late as 1970. In the areas of Hadoti Anchal and Keshavrai Patan in Bundi district, the 'devadasis' were known as 'bhagtans'. These 'bhagtans' who had been donated as offerings by their poor parents, usually performed in the Manik Chowk of Keshavrai temple. Richly bejewelled in silver and gold ornaments and owning about three thousand 'bighas' of land, they danced in the temple not only to the Krishna devotee, Keshavdas, but also in the 'rath-yatras' (chariot journeys). These 'bhagtans' did not entertain people in their homes but instead, 'rasikas' had to come to their performances. At the beginning of the twentieth century, Kesar, Kasturi, Saubhag, Vilas, Lad Kanwar Nanda, Ganeshi and Phoola were some of the well-known 'bhagtans'.

Poses and Stances

The existence of a full-fledged dance right from 900 BC in the region of the Indus-Gangetic belt cannot be denied. Pre-historic cave paintings and figures and figurines of the pre-Christian era point towards the 'natural vertical stance' of the dancers. Curvatures in the body stances as also seen in frescoes and carved friezes came into vogue with later-day developments. All dance forms, initially in the vertical stance, later developed into distinct forms in the post-Christian era. In the Indus-Gangetic belt, there was, however, a continuing almost vertical stance of the dance form, that is reminiscent of Kathak. A sweeping glance at the enormous wealth of carved railings, sculptures and frescoes that are available from the neolithic and paleolithic period and third millennium BC to about the 13th century AD would indicate that the outward bend of the knees were not so important in the representations upto the 6th-

7th century AD. This aspect dominates the sculptures of the period especially around the tenth to the thirteenth centuries AD. The sculptural evidences establish the continuity in the basic form of dance, from the ancient times to the present-day practice. As bards or story-tellers (Kathaks), the dance form while assuming definite contours in terms of 'angas' (body movements), 'caris' (gaits), 'hastas' (hand gestures) and expression, sought to depict the perfect point or movement of balance along the 'brahmasutra' (vertical median) concerning itself in direct relation to the pull of gravity. The dance form developed greater stylisation in terms of rhythmic movement and mime as it became part of social life. In order to study the stances and poses adopted in the various sculptural pieces or in painting representations, it is necessary to understand the hallmarks of Kathak:

- a near vertical stance
- naturalistic, as distinct from the exaggerated, use of 'tribhangi' and the 'ardhamandali' positions
- usage of 'pataka', 'adhomukha', 'hansapaksha', 'hansasya', 'alapadma', 'arala', 'sarpasirsa', 'swastika', 'dola', 'samputa' and 'puspaputa hastas' predominantly in the 'nritta' segments.

Sculptures reflect the dance forms as they might have been prevalent or might have existed during a specific period. Some of the stances and poses exhibited in the sculptures could be universally applicable to all dance forms; however, in order to relate the sculpture's poses and stances to a particular dance form, the historical thread of continuity through which a sculpture evolves into, perhaps, a more complex form in a particular region , has to be taken into consideration. It is in this thread of continuous evolution that a practicing dance form of a region should be contextualised, reflecting the ethos of the sculptural traditions of the area.

In the pre-Mauryan period, the figurines of the dancer from Harappa and Mohenjo-daro reveal that the basic stance of the dance was on vertical lines with hardly any angular

The 'laughing nati'.

An example of pirouette in Kathak.

exaggeration of the torso, hip and knees. The hand movements are natural. The stance adopted by the dancers of the Mauryan empire indicate certain likèness of poses to the Kathak of today. A glance at the statue of the 'laughing nati' (3rd century BC) discovered by Mr. Jackson in 1912 at Patliputra, shows a striking resemblance to a Kathak artiste in a moment during a execution of the pirouette. A comparison with a modern day Kathak artiste would reveal similarities in upper hand and leg positions including the flared state of the skirt. The 'nati' statues of Patlipura of 3rd century BC are similar to Kathak poses in their natural vertical stance and the manner of holding the arms with

Two examples of a aancer from Pataliputra.

the feet in the 'samapada' position. The figures of the 'yakshis' and 'apsaras' from Patliputra, Bharhut, Sanchi, Kausambi, Mathura, Jhusi, Bodh Gaya and Deoghar also indicate dance movements practised in that region. Some of the recesses in the ruins of Nalanda show dancing 'apsaras' in poses not unsimilar to the ones used in Kathak. Similarly, the steatite plaque exhumed at Rajgir, depicts through the

Dancer from Kosambi.

carvings in the three registers, the social life and custom of
the period replete with music and dance. The top register
depicts a man in a dhoti playing a harp while the lady, in
a dancing pose with a vertical stance, has her right hand
raised in the 'uttarkarana' and the left hand in the
'adhomukha hastaka' respectively. The Bharhut panel (west
gate corner of the Ajatsatru pillar) representing nymphs and

A panel of dancers and musicians from Deogarh; fifth century.

dancers dancing to the accompaniment of music in the
'paradise of Indra' is revealing for the poses and feet positions
used. The predominant position of the dancing figures in
these panels is vertical with only a very naturally slight
outward bend of the knees of one leg. The hand movements
are on simplistic lines. The first and third dancers in the

panel from the left have their right arms in a stretched lower position with the left arms near the ear and the feet in a crossed position in one and in an outstretched position with a slight bend in the knee in the other. Most of the dancers have one arm near the ear in a 'pataka hasta'. In subsequent years, the 'hasta' (hand gesture) near the ear was lowered to the bust level. If raised to the forehead, the

Dancers and nymphs from the Bharut panel.

pose formed corresponds to the 'chhapka' (head ornament) movement. Another figure in the panel with the two hands joined together at the centre can be traced to the 'tatkar' movement, a third to the outward 'thai' movement (elongated hand movement). This panel also reveals the presence of a musician playing an elongated drum.

In the second Bharhut panel (outer face of Prasanajit pillar), while two positions of the dancers have been repeated, of the other two dancers, one has both the hands in 'pataka hastas' near the neck. If lowered slightly, the dynamic movement of the hands are utilised within the rendering of 'thaat' and 'amad' in Kathak. The movement of the fourth dancer with outstretched hands over the head finds echoes

Yet another example from the Bharut panel.

in the 'udan' movement.

The figures of 'yaksh' and 'yakshi' from the Bharhut panels again emphasise their almost vertical stance. The sinuous outline of the arms, the right being raised above the head while the left being directed towards the thighs, suggest graceful rhythm in the movement. Even though

Dancing couple from Mathura.

these figures of 'devatas', 'yakshis' and 'salabhanjikas' are strictly not related to dance, they are, however, significant for an indication of the placement of feet and the postures used which can be illustrative of the art traditions in the area. In *Le theatre Indien*, Sylvain Levi describes the dramatic recitation of the Kathaks. He defines the dance sequences as given in the Sanchi bas-reliefs of the pre-Christian era. Schlagintweit, in his lithograph *Kathak-tanzer* from his *Indien in Wort und Bild* refers to an indistinct photograph of a sculptured panel at Sanchi which is said to represent a female entertainer dancing before a king. He also says, 'the modern representatives of the ancient Indian court actor are the Kathaks.... Their discourse takes the shape of an artistic declamation supported by gesticulations. Song and dignified graceful dance fill the pauses.'

Arthur Beriedale Keith, in his Sanskrit Drama, says: 'Fortunately, we have in a bas-relief from Sanchi, which may safely be placed before the Christian era, a presentation of a group of these Kathaks.'

The reliefs of Sanchi, Deoghar and Mathura are characteristic of naturalism and spontaneity of movement while also being representative of the 'thaat ang', the 'angrai ang', 'svastika cari' (crossed feet position) where the weight of the body was on one leg, the other being free to move and also the 'parsva' (side) movement near the waist, thereby being a mirror of restraint, precision and grace. The terracotta figurines of dancers from Kausambi (second and first centuries BC) and the dancing couple from Mathura (first century AD) reflect naturalness of movements. Even the terracotta figure from Manipuri (5th century AD) and the headless dancing woman from Jhusi are examples of the directness of approach of the Gupta period with a flowing sense of beauty and rhythm even while maintaining the vertical stance of the position with no great deflections. Jhusi has been identified as Pratishthanpur of ancient India.

The possibility of more wealth of information emanating from this area has been indicated by Sir Mortimer Wheeler writing in *Ancient India.*

The sculptures of some of the 'apsaras' at the Vaman temple of Khajuraho, the figures in the Tejpal temple at Mount Abu, Telika Mandir, Gwalior, and the temples at Mathura, reveal the existence of a highly developed dance

The headless dancing woman from Jhusi.

form in ancient India in the Indo-Gangetic belt and the adjacent areas with identifying links to the present day Kathak. The sixth century figures of the 'dancing Kartikeya' found at Gaya shows the 'tribhangi' movement as though caught in a moment of dynamism and being frozen in time by the sculptor. The 'hastas' (hand gestures) used were simplistic.

The sculptures of the later date temples of Rajasthan and Allahabad, indicate certain variations in the stance of the dancer. While continuing the near vertical median of the body and the 'samapada sthan' and the 'svastika cari' of the feet with the accompanying natural hip deflection and 'kshipta' bend of the knees, the use of the 'urdhvajanu' placement of the feet with raised knees is evident. This was a period where sculptures from all regions saw flights of imagination of the sculptor not only in forms but also in the use of the human body, highlighting the beauty of the physical form and the display of 'tantric' philosophy through erotic art. The ideas centering around the potent phallus symbol as a recognition of the world coming into being through the union of the male and female gained ground. This interpretation of the sacredness of the physical aspect, 'bhoga' (tasting of earthly pleasures to seek union) as against 'yoga' (prayer of contemplation) gave certain sanctions and liberties to the artistes of the renaissance period in order to bring sensuality and refinement to their art. This trend along with the use of 'urdhavajanu' stance seems to have been discontinued shortly after it was evident from the later date reliefs and paintings from the regions of Rajasthan, Kangra, etc.

In the ancient period the tradition of frescoes and paintings co-existed even while sculptures came to prominence. A glance at the pre-historic wall paintings in the Bhimbedka caves and Singanpur caves in Madhya Pradesh and the paleolithic paintings discovered near Mirzapur indicate dance forms which mirrored the natural stances adopted in real life.

With the establishment of Muslim rule in India, sculpture gave way to painting as any hint of iconography did not blend well with the tenets of Islamic thought.

During the Pala period, some evidences of mural paintings in Bihar have been discovered in the excavated ruins at Nalanda from the Serai mound. Amongst the figures is one of a dancer in a vertical stance, wearing a close fitting bodice.

The painting tradition from the twelfth century to the eighteenth century also provides considerable insight into the form of dance prevailing in the area through the ages, providing an invaluable continuity to the tradition such as the paintings in the Madanpur temple in Jhansi as distinct from the paintings of the later Mughal period. The paintings of the Gujarat school (11th-16th centuries with emphasis on Jain manuscripts as well as themes based on the love of Radha and Krishna), and the Rajasthani school (16th-18th centuries on themes relating to Radha-Krishna, Shiva-Parvati, ragmalas), offer visual visual representation to the emotional states of mind. The 'Pahari' school (including Kangra) again centering around the eternal theme of Krishna and his love-episodes with Radha, and the Mughal school especially of the later period where music and dance in the courts were portrayed through singular tenderness and lyrical grace, held up a mirror to the dance form prevalent in those times. The dance performed by the dancing girls hailing from the court of Baz Bahadur before the Mughal Emperor Akbar, in the Akbarnamah, has been identified as Kathak by the authorities of the Victoria and Albert Museum. Similarly, the paintings of the dancing scene 'samgrahini sutra' of the sixteenth century depicting a dancing girl in a short blouse, skirt with bare midriff and tight pyjamas in the court of Baz Bahadur and in the procession at the court of Akbar in the Padishahnama series, are clearly Kathak.

Even though some of the paintings and earlier sculptures may show evidence of 'ardhamandali' or the 'tribhangi' positions yet these are not unknown within Kathak and the Ras. Thus, foot movements and positions corresponding to 'ardhamandali', 'svastika' etc. form part of dynamic movements such as while playing a 'pakhawaj' (drum) or while denoting the 'devi' (a goddess). However, the increasing virtuosity in the demonstration of footwork and

pirouettes which reached newer heights of excellence and
demanded equal balance of weight on both feet while
maintaining a vertical axis for acquiring greater speed and
momentum, automatically shifted the emphasis in the body
posture. Similarly, the 'abhanga' and the 'tribhangi' positions
utilised by Kathak dancers while denoting Krishna or Radha
carrying water pitchers on her waist, are camouflaged by
the loose flowing costume of the dancer.

The art of painting was highly mature in Patna and
one of the frequently treated subject was dance. From 1760
onwards, the Kayastha artistes from Murshidabad moved to
Patna. The paintings of Sewak Ram (1770-1830) depicted
various dancing girls thereby portraying Indian occupations
of the kind that generally appealed to the British. The
Patna school of paintings (the Patna Kalam) shows a clear
departure from ordinary Mughal usage in the illustration
of literature depicting of court life. The paintings of Hulas
Lal (1785-1875) again depict groups of dancing girls not
unlike those of Sewak Ram. A water colour painting by
Shiv Lal (1817-1877) shows a gentleman being entertained
by dancing girls. This was apparently painted by him in
1860 and now hangs in the Victoria and Albert museum.
Painting on mica of lady musicians attributed to Shiv Dayal
Lal (1820-1880) was done by him in 1865 approximately
and also hangs in the Victoria and Albert museum. One of
the asistants of Shiv Dayal Lal, by the name of Jamuna
Prasad (1859-84), has painted dancing girls wearing pink
and blue blouses.

Yaadgar-e-rozgar, an Urdu work by Syed Badrul Hasan,
senior honorary magistrate at the Patna city court, describes
Patna at the turn of the century. This work contains
sketches of famous courtesans of Patna who were experts
in the field of music and dance. Some of these courtesan
dancers became the subject of painters of the Patna Kalam.
Interestingly, the poses adopted by the dancers, as depicted

in these paintings, were extremely natural holding a vertical stance. This is not surprising as they had been initiated into the art of Kathak. It follows that there is an identifying link in the 'angas' and 'angikas' of the dance prevalent in this region right from 900 BC till today, portraying social life, dance form, concept of beauty and musical instruments prevalent in that period. Also conceding the fact that most of the temples and other specimens of architecture of this region have not survived till today, yet the few remaining sculptural and painting evidences, throw light on the gamut of poses used in the dance form through the ages.

Classical Dance Forms

Deliberating on the form and stances adopted by the different classical dance styles in relation to the available temple sculptures depicting dancing postures, a number of questions come to mind. Did the near vertical stance of kathak influence the sculptors of the area or were the dancers influenced by the sculptors? Was the 'tribhangi' of the Odissi derived from sculptured panels or was it just the reverse? The answer, perhaps, may be somewhere in the middle. Imagination plays a key role in the creative output of an artist whether he is a dancer or a sculptor or painter. While giving form to his art, the artist may resort to exaggeration in order to bring out the mood of the subject. In dance, the basic stances adopted were exaggerated versions of real life stances, though not to the extent as shown in paintings or sculptures.

To begin with, drama, music and dance were integral parts of theatre not unsimilar to an opera, operetta or a 'nautanki' of today. The emotional process occurring during any dance performance transports the dancer and the audience into a realm of beauty binding them together in the thread of 'rasa' (bliss). All dance forms originating as the outward expression of a deep religious sentiment and ending with the taste of 'rasa', are similar in their origins and ultimate aims. It is only the regional development which has given each dance form its characteristic flavour. The dancer's personality and her aesthetic and spiritual involvement cannot be set aside. Nardas, in his *Sangita Makaranda*, defines the attributes of a dancer as—

*ange 'na lamba ye'gditam haste, nartham pradarshayet,
netrabhyam bhavyedhatam padabhyam tala nirnayal.*

(by his body he indicated the general import of a song, with his hands its meaning; with his eyes he expresses the feelings and sentiments and with his feet he keeps the time.)

The plurality of dance forms could be compared to the various streams of the river, having a similar origin but traversing different paths in their voyage to mingle with the mighty ocean and rest in its tranquility. Our dance forms, originating from belief and worship of '*ananda - dhyana - vishwas*', traverse the experience of 'rasa' before attaining the sublime bliss of 'moksha'. Even in terms of the mood generated, all the dance forms attempt to transport the performers and the audience to a level of spiritual bliss.

In keeping with the theory of thesis-antithesis-synthesis, evolving from a loose-limbed dance form in a naturalistic stance to narrate stories about the Lord or to sing his praise, the practice of narration through dance spread to remote corners of the country, only to coalesce into distinct postures to become distinctive dance forms. In the process, the basic

stance adopted by each form became the fulcrum from which
emanated various other movements and the types of gaits
and foot contacts with the earth.

While Bharatnatyam and Kuchipudi saw the 'ardhmandali'
or the half sitting position with the heels pressed together
as the basic stance, Odissi, Kathakali and Mohiniattam had
incorporated a similar body posture but with the feet placed
apart. In direct contrast, Kathak from the Gangetic belt
continued with the naturalistic near vertical stance of the
body with the feet placed together. The basic posture struck
by the Manipuri dancers lies somewhere between Kathak
and the other forms.

As far as the vertical positioning of the body is concerned
or the body's position from the torso upwards, Bharatnatyam,
Kathak and Kathakali predominantly use the 'samabhanga'
(the vertical position) or the 'abhanga' (with one deflection
resulting in a slightly imbalanced position). This does not
mean that the 'tribhanga' (with two deflections when the
body can be divided into three distinct parts) is not
employed in these dance forms or that the Odissi form
utilises only the 'tribhangi'. However, 'tribhanga' is utilised
to a very great extent by Odissi dancers, thus lending the
form its own characteristic flavour. Similarly, the 'ardhmandali'
or the 'urdhvajanu' (one leg lifted up from the knees) are
employed in Kathak and Manipuri, not as basic static
positions but in transitory motion making them dynamic
movements. While 'mrigasirsa hastas' are employed in
Bharatnatyam with the feet crossed, the hind foot supporting
the weight of the body which is itself in a slight 'tribhanga'
position and a slight tilt of the head, the Kathak artiste
would employ two 'katakamukha hastas' for the flute and
also stand with the feet crossed but with the front foot
supporting the weight of the body which again is in a
slightly 'tribhanga' position with a slight tilt of the head.
'Singamukha mudra' of the flute is supported by the body

adopting a very sharp 'tribhangi' position involving a sharply pronounced 'atibhang' in the Odissi style. Thus, a combination of the torso posture the feet placement along with the positioning of the body helps in the identification of a dance form.

Kathak perceives the body along the central vertical median, not far removed from life itself with the three-dimensional effect emerging through dynamic motion. In characteristic poses resembling the postures adopted by the 'salabhanjikas' of the various sculptures, the slight 'tribhangi' deflection of the body gets camouflaged under the loose-flowing robes, whether it be the 'lehenga' (ankle-length skirt) or the full-skirted 'angarkha' unlike the costumes of Bharatnatyam or Odissi which emphasise even the slightest curve of the body. The weight of the body is equally divided on both feet with a very slight flexing of the knees. While moving forward, the placement of the 'ancita' foot (heel on the ground) before the entire foot is firmly placed is extremely subtle leaving the impression of placement of foot as though in real life. Similarly, in moving backwards, the usage of 'kunchita' foot (placing of toe on the ground) is so subtle that the picture of movement or the flat foot carrying the weight of the body emerges. However, in the 'gat sequence', the 'kuncita' foot is repeatedly used to move forward, backward or sideways.

In Bharatnatyam, the body position emerges as triangles with the shoulders to the waist forming an inverted triangle. The second triangle is conceived from the waist to the outstretched knees while the third triangle is conceived through the outstretched knees to the heels placed together.

Kuchipudi largely follows the same pattern and positioning but with a certain springiness in the gait. In Kathakali, though largely following the 'ukkara' position for the knees, yet the feet are kept apart with the soles of the feet touching the ground in the position known as the 'mandalasthana'. The dancer moves in rectangles and squares with clear extensions of the leg.

Odissi adopts the 'chowk' with its outstretched knees in the 'ardhamandali' position and the feet placed apart, yet it differs from the other forms in that that the body is invariably given a 'tribhangi' or the 'natwarbhangi' treatment in which the hip is given a sharp deflection leading the torso to tilt in the opposite direction while the head is deflected on the same side as the hip. Such sharp hip deflections are not visibly practised in other dance forms.

Manipuri from the north-eastern region is very different from all the other dance forms. Even though this dance follows a near vertical stance of the body, yet this stance flows from the 'samabhanga' to the 'abhanga' and the 'tribhanga' position with such ease, thus imparting to it a dynamic fluidity and grace. Sharp deflection of the body is totally unheard of in Manipuri. The feet starting from a 'samapada' position moves in a serpentine gait with a corresponding movement of the body and hands, giving the effect of drawing fluid pictures of eight or Ss, through controlled movements of all parts of the body.

Amongst all the classical dance forms, Kathak maintains the most natural body stance emphasising the dynamic aspect of nature and life. The common impulse to externalise those states into movements which otherwise is latent within is the basic principle underlying Kathak. The movements, gestures and postures are drawn from everyday life and the emotions expressed by the dancer are immediately identifiable by the spectator despite certain phrases of abstraction and formalisation that is inherent in any classical dance form.

Broadly speaking, the format of presentation highlighting the 'nritta', 'nritya' (associated with mime) and 'natya' (dramatic) aspects can be classified as invocation, pure rhythmic sequences with musical accompaniment, expressional or mime pieces (with or without interspersed rhythmic patterns) and melodic-rhythmic pieces as the finale. Invocation may be done through the 'alarippu' in Bharatnatyam, 'cholkettu' in Mohiniattam, 'shloka' or 'vandana' in Kathak and Manipuri, 'mangalacharan' or 'bighnaraj puja' in Odissi and 'todayam' or 'purappad' in Kathakali. The pure rhythmic sequence include the 'jatisvaram' in Bharatnatyam and Mohiniattam, 'thaat', 'amad', 'tore', 'tukre' in Kathak, the 'kirtiprabandh' or 'swarmala' in Manipuri, the 'pallavi', 'swarpallavi' or 'batu nritya' in Odissi and the 'adakkam' or 'tomakaram' in Kathakali. As regards Manipuri, the repertoire includes the 'lai haroba' and the 'khamba thoibi' as pure dance sequences with expression while the various 'cholam' dances and the 'thanghaiba' and 'takhew-saiba' are rhythmic, virile and acrobatic in nature.

The expressional sequences are the 'sabdam', 'varnam' and 'padam' in Bharatnatyam, the 'gat-bhava', 'gat-nikas', 'thumri', 'dhrupad', 'dhamar', 'bhajan', 'geet' and 'gazal' in Kathak, the 'batu nritya', 'gitabhinaya' and the 'sabhinaya' in Odissi and the 'rasa' dances (maharasa, basantrasa, kunjrasa and the nityarasa) of Manipuri. In Kathakali the story is enacted by the characters. Here, the basic nine moods, the full gamut of expression and a variety of hand gestures are utilised by the dancers of all dance forms in order to mime the story.

For the finale, the 'tillana' followed by a 'sloka' are performed in Bharatnatyam and Mohiniattam, 'tarangam' in Kuchipudi while the Kathak repertoire includes the 'tarana', 'chaturang', 'adana', 'sargam' and the 'tatkar'. The 'telena' or the 'chaturang' in Manipuri, the 'tarajan' and 'moksha' in Odissi and the final sloka in Kathakali are executed as finale pieces.

Interestingly, while dancing on a brass plate still exists as part of 'tarangam' in a Kuchipudi recital, such an item which had formed a small part of the Kathak repertoire of the Jaipur and Benaras 'gharanas' in earlier times has now been dispensed with.

All classical dance forms in India though born in the
temples of different regions of the country, incorporated
and displayed the rhythmic (nritta) and expressional (nritya)
aspects while the dramatic (natya) was predominant in the
more theatrical styles. The dance forms in the format as
seen today were formalised only during the last 300-400
years.

Most of the seven classical dance forms are story-telling,
soloistic dance forms necessitating the use of 'hastakas' (hand
gestures), body movements and facial emotions in the
delineation of the story, emphasising the individualistic skill
and artistry of the artiste. The themes enacted by the dancers
are taken from Hindu mythological stories. The 'Dasavatara'
enumerating the 10 incarnations of Lord Vishnu, various
episodes taken from the Ramayana featuring Rama, Sita,
Ravana, Lakshman and Hanuman and from the Krishna-leela
featuring Lord Krishna and Radha and various episodes from
the religious epic, the Mahabharata, verses from the various
vedas and upanishads, teachings of saints and sages and the
various states of a maiden in love enumerated in the 'ashta-
nayika' and devotional songs are the common sources of
'abhinaya' for all the Indian classical dance-forms.

On the historical front, all Indian classical dance forms
share some similarity in their phases of development. Temples
were the places of origin where the dancers or the priests
danced in praise of the Lord enacting various mythological
stories. The system flourished under the patronage given by
the rulers and society at large. However, with exploitation
(often sexual in so far as women dancers were concerned),
the art forms degenerated and so did the status of dancers
in all parts of India. In certain areas, due to political changes,
social customs underwent a sea change and all the dance
forms regressed, surfacing only when a local ruler or zamindar
displayed a personal interest in patronising the art form in
all areas of his domain. In some areas that remained

untouched by Muslim rule, a large number of dancers performed in the temples and the courts patronised by the local ruler, the priests and society at large. As a result of the social renaissance initiated in the last two centuries, the 20th century too witnessed a cultural renaissance. Not only did the dance forms and their practitioners regain their old glorified status but many innovations and inter-regional and cross-cultural influences were seen resulting in further development within the various forms.

In medieval India when Muslim rule held sway, the veil which had been adopted by society has often been cited as one of the primary reasons for confining the various dance forms to the temples. However, a comparison of the areas under Muslim rule with those areas which did not see Muslim rule, predominantly in the southern regions of India, show that in all these regions, dance remained confined to the temples revealing a strong presence of the brahminical tradition and a common social norm.

As long as dance was taken to be mere entertainment, there was a predominance of women dancers in the courts; but when dance became more cogent or when the attitude of the patron changed to a deep abiding interest in the art form, then the sex of the artiste became immaterial. It is perhaps due to this that Kathak and male performers (who had till then been temple dancers) came to the limelight during the reign of Nawab Wajid Ali Shah. The Nawab gave a fillip to the art-form, sowed the seeds of the Lucknow 'gharana' (Lucknow school of dance) and raised the artistry of dance. Similar contributions were made by the Hindu rulers of Rajasthan and Eastern Uttar Pradesh. The 20th century, especially the later part, has seen the dance canvas dotted with many women and male dancers with the former outnumbering the latter mainly because of social acceptance and psychological conditioning in favour of dance today.

Kathak and the Shastras

On the issue whether the *Natyashastra* is as applicable to Kathak as to any other dance form, an analysis of the various body movements (gaits, jumps, leaps, spins and usage of the hand gestures, eye, brow, neck movements and the moods) are called for. Chapters xiv, xviii, xxii and xxiii of the *Natyashastra* cover the length and breadth of India with references to geographical areas, tribes, and languages. There are references to Anga (north Bihar), Antargiri (Himalayan region), Avanti (M.P.), Kashmir, Nepal, Panchal, Kasi, Kosala (Uttar Pradesh), Videh (Bihar), Magadh (Bihar), Sindhu (north-western state), Bhargava (Gujarat), Maharashtra, Malaya (Karnataka), Vindhya, Andhra, Brahmottra (Bay of Bengal), Tripura, Dravida,. Surastra (Gujarat), Saurasena (UP), etc. There are references to the tribes and their languages such as Kasi, Kosala, Barbara, Abhira, Dramida, Sabara, Saka, Andhra, Candala, Pallava and Yavana to name a few. Thus, all in all, this treatise lays down a codification of all aspects of dramaturgy as found throughout the subcontinent.

In the *Natyashastra*, the origin of dance, its evolution and dissemination centered around the Himalayan belt. At the instance of Lord Indra, Lord Brahma created the fifth veda: the *Natyaveda*. Veda is knowledge derived from the word 'vid', i.e. to know. For the *Natyaveda*, 'word' was taken from the *Rigaveda*, 'music' from *Samaveda*, 'histrionics' from *Yajurveda* and 'rasa' (emotions) from the *Atharvaveda*. Bharata staged a production called 'asura parajaya' dealing with the defeat and destruction of the asuras or demons. This offended the demons. Thereafter, Lord Brahma formalised the theatrical production and explained the nature and purpose of 'natya' (drama). When the production attained perfection, two plays, 'Amritmanthan' and 'Tripuradaha' were presented before Lord Shiva at Kailash. Shiva suggested incorporation of dance and ordained Sage Tandu to teach 'nritta' (pure dance) to Bharata. Soon after, pleased with their success, the disciples of Bharata, called 'Bharatas', became arrogant and incurred the wrath of the sages and deities. They were cursed that their 'living shall be dependent on the patronage of the public and by the sale of talent and art'. Sometime later, King Nahush of Pratishthanpur sought introduction of 'natya vidya' (dramatic knowledge) in his kingdom. Bharata accepted his suggestion and sent his disciples to the earth, thus spreading the art of music, dance and theatre in that region. (Pratishthanpur has been identified as the area near Jhusi on the Ganges near Prayag.)

The *Natyashastra* dwells in detail on the discussion of the various aspects of such a production. With the passage of time, drama, music and dance developed in individual streams coalescing together to give rise to various forms and schools within each stream of art. This was the genesis of the various forms of folk and classical dance traditions.

The differences between the classical and folk arts may be broadly classified as follows:

I)   classical dance requires individual skill, excellence, and detailed training.

II)   classical dance presupposes the existence of a viewer and a performer whereas folk dance is participative in nature.

III) folk dance is instinctive and impulsive with an inherent spontaneous joy whereas classical dance is ruled by intellect.

IV)   classical dance stems from the works of individuals, appealing to the senses and stimulating the intelligence of performer and spectator alike.

V)   classical dance utilises highly evolved body movements and hand language.

In the context of known scholarly works on art traditions, there was a consolidation of information on the theatrical traditions in India. The *Ashtadhyayi* of Patanjali and Silalin's *Natasutra* refer to the 'nata' or the 'dancer'; however, the definition of the term given by Panini is closer to the interpretation of 'nata' as the 'professional dancer' even though a clear distinction between the 'nata' and the 'nartaka' has not been provided by Panini himself.

The language of dance employs a standardisation of gestures, body positions, gaits and emotions, dependent on the universality of gestures which is amply reflected in the various treatises such as the *Natyashastra*, the *Abhinaya Darpan* and the *Sri Hastamuktavali*. Of these, the *Natyashastra* occupies a place of pride being the first and the oldest as well as the most comprehensive written manuscript available (the other treatises dwell in detail on some specific aspects of theatre or dance). The *Natyashastra*, written sometime between the second century BC and second century AD is a treatise comprising all aspects of dramatology covering various aspects of drama, music and dance. It was the living art traditions (folk and classical) practised in the various regions of India that enabled the compilation of such a monumental work. All stances, movements, gaits, hand gestures, moods, pirouettes, etc. that are inevitable limbs of all dances (folk and classical) may be traced in this compilation. Bharata has been credited with the authorship of the *Natyashastra*; but there are some scholars who opine that the *Natyashastra* had been written in parts by different authors at different periods of time and that it was one great scholar amongst them, an adept in the science of drama, who had probably compiled and connected the various written materials and presented it as the *Natyashastra* under the authorship of Bharata. It was only with the passage of time that the authorship of Bharata as the author was established due to its antiquity and the reference given by Kalidasa in his play Vikramorvasiya. The period of Kalidas is taken to be around 400 AD.

Hindu mythology is replete with tales about gods and goddesses, more often than not being represented as an artiste in any situation. Not surprisingly, such myths form the repertoire of all our dance forms, besides being a major factor in their origin. Temples sprang up where the devotees gathered to pray to the Almighty God or hear stories about Him. Within the portals of its courtyard, some of the devotees sang and danced in praise of the Lord, while in some temples, the priests themselves narrated mythological tales through dance. From simplistic nuances and movements, they developed into full-fledged art forms thus laying the foundation for the classical dance forms that we see in India today.

In the Indian context the term 'classical' also denotes adhering to the principles of the 'Shastras' (treatise on the codification of the various arts); in other words, there is an inherent spirit of Sanskritisation. But while conforming to the treatises of *Natyashastra*, Kathak has not confined itself to Sanskritisation alone, reflecting instead the vibrant spirit of the area.

The Kathak, as a solo dancer, who danced and sang in praise of the Lord describing Him and His qualities and relating anecdotes from His life, drew no support from other Kathaks and, therefore, the language of hand gestures along with 'caris' and 'angas' (feet and body movements respectively) and 'bhavas' and 'abhinaya' (moods and expressions) assume great importance. Every action was significant and thereby evolved a myriad gestures. This, therefore, is the 'ekapatraharya lasyanga' mentioned in the *Natyashastra* whereby the solo dancer enacts and interprets the story or theme with the help of four 'abhinayas' (expressions): the 'angika' (body movements including hand gestures and facial expressions), 'vacikabhinaya' (singing or reciting a text), 'aharyabhinaya' (use of costume, make-up, stage props) and the 'sattvikabhinaya' (expressing the appropriate emotional and psychological conditions).

The dance itself, can be divided into distinct parts: the 'nritya' (expressional, mimetic), the 'nritta' (pure rhythmic portion) and the 'natya' (dramatic). The term 'natya' is an imitation of a condition where 'rasa' (aesthetic emotion) is the expression. The word, therefore, is not strictly a derivative of 'natak' (drama). Thus, inclusion of the 'natya' to the dance form gives it substance. 'Nritya' combines ideas of dancing and acting while interpreting a story or the lines of a text (sahitya). In the delineation of these aspects, the 'rasa' or the aesthetic emotion charges the atmosphere radiating 'ananda' (bliss) while in union with the Lord. Even within the execution of dance, the virility or the grace with which the pieces are danced have been classified into the 'tandava' and the 'lasya' respectively. In a simplified explanation, the energetic and virile display of dance is stated to represent the cosmic activities, the 'tandava'; while the narration about the Gods, the 'lasya'; yet even in the 'nritta' and 'nritya' portions, the dance delineations could be 'tandava' or 'lasya' respectively.

The Kathak dance form includes within its framework positions of the body which are largely confined to natural movements. Unnatural positions of the limbs and exaggerated movements of the hips are not deployed resulting in an easy manoeuvrability of the body and the feet. While natural grace is maintained, the basic stance of the body lends itself to complexities in footwork and the ability of the feet and body to perform at a breathtaking tempo.

Performing the 'tatkar', the 'chakkars' or 'bhramaris' (pirouettes) at a great tempo is possible only because of the near vertical stance of the body which maintains the balance and provides the momentum.

The basic feet positions include 'mandala' (posture), 'utplavana' (leaping movement or jumping), 'bhramari' (flight circular movement) and 'cari' (gait).

Some of the basic positionings of the feet frequently deployed in Kathak are:

Sampada Sthan: In this posture the feet are placed together in a flat position with the toes pointing a little outwards. This position lends itself to a number of poses while also forming the starting position before the commencement of a rhythmic pattern.

Asvakranta Sthan: Here while one foot is in the normal position the other foot is raised on its toes. When the two feet are crossed as in svastika, it helps depict postures such as those of Lord Krishna, Radha, Vishnu, etc.

Avahittha Sthan: In this position the feet are placed slightly apart with one being in the normal position and the other in a crossed position. This would, in any case, have a corresponding influence on the opposite hip by raising it slightly.

Alidha Sthan: The feet are placed slightly apart with the right foot forward. In this position, there are three basic subdivisions. In the first, the weight of the body is resting on the left foot. In the second position, the weight of the body is on the right foot, while in the third position the right foot is in a bent position and supports the weight of the body. Similarly, the three positionings of the feet bent with the left foot forward is known as *pratyalidha sthan.* These positions are commonly used while striking the *sama* (the finale of the rhythmic pattern).

Swastika Sthan: In yet another position commonly used, specially while denoting Lord Shiva, the left foot is placed firmly on the ground while the right foot is raised high above the ground crossing the left knee.

In the Natwari Krishna, the dancing Krishna with the pakhawaj (drum), the stance used is the *mandal sthan* in which the feet are placed wide apart and the knees are slightly bent in the opposite direction. The same positioning of the feet is used within the dance form but with the right foot or the left foot placed backwards.

In the *Ayata Sthan,* one foot is in the normal position and the heel of the other foot is stretched and raised.

As far as the movement of the feet is concerned, some of the various usages are as follows:

The feet are placed together and alternatively one foot is raised and struck flat on the ground (sama). The second movement of the feet include raising of the heels and striking back on the ground with the heel (udghatita). The third variety includes striking on the ground with the side of the feet as in the ghi-na-dha foot work. The fourth usage includes moving on the toes with the heels raised (agratala sanchar). The 'ancita' movement refers to moving on the heels while the 'kuncita' movement is used with the arching of the sole. One foot in the 'sama' (flat) position sliding along and the other foot in the 'agratal sanchar' with heels raised and striking the ground with the toe in quick succession are normally employed while ending of the 'gat nikas' (gait) sequence.

The 'khiskan' movement is performed in two ways. In the first alternative, the heels of the feet and then the toes meet together in quick succession while covering space in a sliding manner. In the second alternative, the feet slide parallel to each other.

The 'kridha' movement raises the body above the ground with both feet for a split of a second and coming back to earth on the toes of one foot and the second foot simultaneously striking the earth with the heel and then with both the feet coming to rest in the final 'sama' position. In another forward movement (chal) the ground is alternatively struck with the heel and flat of the two feet.

In the 'thararara' movement, the toe is pressed against the ground and moved backward to forward, giving a continuous ringing sound. Similarly, the reclining body positions such as the 'prasarita' and the 'vivartita' and the numerous sitting positions are utilised in the dance form.

(The feet positions and their movements enumerated above are illustrative and not exhaustive).

The 'bhramaris' or 'chakkars' (pirouettes) have been referred to in the *Natyashastra*, the *Abhinaya Darpana*, the *Nritta Ratnavali* and the *Nritya Ratnakosh*.

> *bhramarya lakshananyatra vakshye lakshanabhedatah*
> *utplutyabhramari cakrabhramari garudabhidha*
> *tathaikapadabhramari kuncitabhramari tatha*
> *akasabhramari ca'va tathangabhramariti ca*
> *bhramaryah saptavigyeya natyasastravisaradaih*

The seven main classifications of the pirouettes are:

* *utpluta bhramari* (to turn with both feet raised)
* *cakra bhramari* (to spin like a top)

- *garuda bhramari* (to turn with one outstretched knee)
- *ekpada bhramari* (to turn on each foot at a time)
- *kuncita bhramari* (to turn with bent knees)
- *akasa* or *utplavana bhramari* (to spin with leaps in the air)
- *anga bhramari* (to turn and freeze in one position)

The other sub-divisions of pirouettes widely used are:

i)	*viparit chakra*	-	taking the first spin from one side and the second spin from the opposite side.
ii)	*ardha chakra*	-	half a spin.
iii)	*ardha viparit chakra*	-	executing half a spin once from the left and then from the left and from the right.
iv)	*kamal chakra*	-	spin in a thrown back position.
v)	*madan chakra*	-	spinning on the knees.

The sub-divisions of 'chakra bhramari' such as the 'viparit chakra' (spin in the opposite direction) and the 'ardh chakra' (half-spin), can be performed in various ways, namely by alternatively placing of the feet to different beats (such as five, three or two) or executing it to the beat of one and the impression conveyed is of a spin. In the 'chakra bhramari' and the 'ekpad bhramari', the left foot is normally maintained as the axis and the momentum is given by striking the right heel. The 'garuda bhramari' and the 'kuncita bhramari' pirouetting on one outstretched knee and bent knees respectively is widely used within the 'rasa' dance form. The 'kamal bhramari' and the 'madan chakra' are performed with the forefoot and both feet respectively while the 'utplavana bhramari' employs pirouettes with leaps. All these varieties of 'bhramaris' are displayed by the performers of Kathak especially belonging to the Jaipur and Benaras 'gharana'.

The pirouette or the 'chakkar' or the 'bhramari' is another characteristic feature of the dance form. The spins are performed with one foot with the body maintaining the axis. The virtuous element can be seen through pirouettes ranging from a couple to as many as twenty-seven or thirty-three or fifty-four, performed continuously at a great speed, without losing balance. The philosophical interpretations of the pirouette range from the revolving of the 'atma' (the soul) around the 'paramatma' (the universal soul) and the 'mandala' (circle) formed by Lord Krishna and the 'gopies' (cow-maidens) in the 'ras-leela' and the 'maharas' to the 'jivan-chakra' and the 'kaal-chakra', the cycle of life and death and the cycle of nature respectively. Even in the 'yantra' and 'tantra', the circle symbolising wholeness occurs very frequently. In the act of becoming, the spiral represents growth symbolised by the flow of electric current and the creative coil of feminine energy or 'kundalini sakti', denoting the inward journey as a microscopic reflection of cosmic rhythms. ('Yantra' is a form or symbol of a geometrical representation of a deity as an aid to contemplation while a 'tantra' is a set of practical ways leading to self-enlightenment especially in the context of 'Shakti' as supreme power.)

The aspect of 'upaj' (innovation, improvisation and creativity) while on stage itself, is a constant demand on the Kathak dancers, as is evident from the rendering of mime especially in the 'bhava batana' and in the rhythmic aspects as borne out by the importance of 'padhant'.

The usual four categories of neck movement are 'sundari' (moving to and fro horizontally), 'tirascina' (upward movement on both sides); 'parivartita' (moving right and left like a slow half-moon) and 'prakampita' (moving backwards and forwards). The six movements of the brows are 'sahaja' (natural), 'patita' (frown), 'utksipta' (one brow being raised), 'chatura' (brows meeting and faintly quivering), 'recita' (one brow being contracted) and 'kuncita' (one or both brows arched). The eight glances (ashta drishti) are: *sama* (level), *alokta* (inspecting), *saci* (sidelong), *pralokita* (turning from side to side), *nimilita* (closed), *ullokita* (looking up), *anuvritta* (following) and *avalokita* (looking down).

Even though the 'rasa' (flavour or aesthetic emotion) is exuded during a dance performance, the 'bhava' (mood or expression) is the first step to the 'rasa' (flavour). The *Natyashastra* has classified human emotions into eight major categories: the mood of 'santam' (peace) was added later as the ninth category. These are 'sringar' (love), 'hasya' (laughter or mirth), 'karuna' (grief), 'roudra' (anger), 'bhaya' (fear), 'vibhatsa' (disgust), 'veer' (valour), 'adbhuta' (wonder) and 'santam' (peace).

The 'abhinaya' (expression) encompasses the 'angika' (bodily), 'vacika' (vocal) and the 'aharya' (ornamental), besides the 'sattvika' (pure). The 'angika' includes the exposition through limbs and the body: 'anga' (i.e. head, hands, feet, neck, etc.), 'pratyanga' (e.g. arms, wrists, knees, etc.) and 'upanga' (e.g. eyes, brows, chin, etc.)

The nine head movements employed are 'sama' (level), 'udvahita' (raised), 'adhomukha' (inclined face), 'alolita' (rolling), 'dhuta' (shaken), 'kampita' (nodding), 'paravratta' (turning aside), 'utkshipta' (turning aside and upwards) and 'parivahita' (moving head from side to side).

The 'hastas' or hand gestures are extensive. The twenty-eight 'asamyukta hastas' or single-hand gestures along with their literal meanings are 'pataka' (flag), 'tripataka' (three parts of a flag), 'ardha-pataka' (half-flag), 'kartarimukha' (arrow shaft), 'mayura' (peacock), 'ardhachandra' (half-moon), 'arala' (bent), 'sukatunda' (parrot's beak), 'musthi' (first), 'sikhara' (spire), 'kapittha' (elephant apple), 'katakamukha' (opening in a chain), 'suci' (needle), 'chandra-kala' (moon), 'padma-kosa' (lotus bud), 'sarpasirsha' (snake-head), 'mrigasirsha' (deer-head), 'simhamukha' (lion-face), 'langula' (tail), 'sola-padma' (full blown lotus), 'catura' (four), 'bhramara' (bee), 'hamsasya' (swan-face), 'hamsapaksha' (swan feather), 'samdamsa' (grasp), 'mukula' (bud), 'tamrachuda' (cock), and 'trisula' (trident). The twenty-four major 'samyukta hastas' or combined hand gestures are 'anjali' (salutation), 'kapota' (dove), 'karkata' (crab), 'svastika' (crossed), 'dola' (swing), 'pushpaputa' (flower casket), 'utsanga' (embrace), 'siva-linga' (phallus), 'kataka-vardhana' (link), 'kartari-svastika' (crossed arrow-shafts), 'sakata' (car), 'sankha' (conch), 'chakra' (disc), 'samputa' (casket), 'pasa' (noose), 'kilaka' (bond), 'matsya' (fish), 'kurma' (tortoise), 'varaha' (boar), 'garuda' (bird), 'naga-bandha' (serpent tie), 'khatva' (bed), 'bherunda' (a variety of birds) and 'avahittha' (dissimulation).

Predominantly, Kathak has eight major features, all of which are represented while performing. These are:

1.	*Ishtapada*	-	prayer and glory to the Lord
2.	*Thaat*	-	introduction of the dance movements and rhythm
3.	*Jatishunya*	-	establishment of the dance movements and expressions
4.	*Gatibhava*	-	enacting a complete story
5.	*Bhavarang*	-	enacting of literary pieces around the hero-heroine
6.	*Nrityang*	-	depiction of the various rhythmic patterns
7.	*Tarana*	-	pure dance sequences (involving musical syllables)
8.	*Tatkar*	-	footwork rising to a crescendo

These features of Kathak exist as self-sufficient and yet very fluid entities. An evening's programme of other dance forms may consist of clearly predefined items with patterns, whereas in the case of Kathak this varies from dancer to dancer. The more mature the dancer, the more fluidity within these features. This is further enhanced through the dancer's direct communication with the audience. In fact, it is this fluidity and the capacity of these features to telescope into each other that places a great responsibility on the Kathak dancer. It is, thus, the dancer's judicious choice of features in application, his/her decision to place them in a rational time rendering that leads to the success of a performance.

In the pure rhythmic sequences danced in succession in a chosen rhythmic cycle for that part of the programme, each pattern is a complete entity by itself exuding its own characteristic flavour according to the vocal and visual imagery and a well-defined body.

A usual Kathak performance would begin with a 'rang-pravesh' namely an entry on to the stage followed by a 'stuti' in praise of the Lord and paying obeisance to the Maker. While the prayer could be a homage to any manifestation of the Lord, quite a few Kathaks preferred to follow it by the 'Ganesh stuti' as Lord Ganesha is symbolic of an auspicious beginning or with a Krishna 'stuti', a Saraswati 'vandana' or a Vishnu 'stuti'. After the entry, a piece is danced which is more in the nature of taking permission of the area within which the performance is to take place and of the accompanying musicians and elders and connoisseurs present in the gathering. During the performance before a Hindu ruler and audience, this was termed as 'rangmach ki pooja' (prayer to the stage) while during the patronage of some selected Mughal nawabs, this was juxtaposed by the 'salami' (i.e. the Muslim form of greetings) in the courts only. The introductory piece which follows the prayer is the 'uthaan' heralding the beginning of the dance.

The 'thaat' which follows the 'uthaan' has been derived from the Hindi word 'thathana' which means to stay in one place. This implies 'thahraav' (to stay still), 'thawan' (stance) and 'thaat-baat' (an allusion to a personality) as in its actual rendering, a stance is adopted where it stays still exuding its characteristic air. Thus, the dancer establishes his or her personality and introduces each and every movement of the eyes, neck, arms, limbs, etc. The attributes of dance as enumerated in the following verse of the *Sangeet Darpan*, namely spark, repose, lining of movements, pirouette, eye glance, pieces which do not induce tiredness, intellect (visible in the rhythmic patterns), meditative spirit, rhythmic utterances and musical notes, are to be found in the delineation of 'thaat' where the verse goes as follows:

*javah sthritvam rekha ca'bhramari drishtirshramah medha
shraddha vacho gitam patra prana dashasmritah*

The 'thaat' is, therefore, a form of 'tantric sadhana' of the practitioner and the Kathak goes through the following four steps in the delineation of 'thaat', namely,

cosmicisation   - subtle removal of outside bodies in a process of sanctification by practice of the correct 'asana' or pose together with breath control and a controlled intonation of the rhythmic syllables.

internalisation   - process in which the spirit of dance becomes part of the self and this state is helped in being achieved through 'mudras', meditative quality, and 'pranayama'.

equilibrium   - achieving a harmonious equilibrium on the physical, psychological and mental planes by regulated physical postures, regulation of breath and internalisation.

self-actualisation - achievement of a state of unity or indivisibility.

The 'amad', the entry which follows, is performed at a slow tempo and set to the mnemonics of dance. '*Amad*' is one of the very few words which could have a non-Indian origin. While it means entry in Persian, the Indian roots of aa + pada, i.e. "step coming towards" or "aagaman" (i.e. to come) cannot be ruled out. The 'toras' and 'tukras' follow suit, which are performed to a slightly increased tempo and are pure rhythmic patterns based on the mnemonics of dance and table (a percussion instrument). The 'natwari' is a rhythmic pattern based on the syllables of dance such as 'ta', 'thai', 'tat', 'digadiga', 'tram' and 'tigada'. The name '*natwari*' it itself derived from the dance of Lord Krishna who is referred as 'Natwar'. It is believed that when he subdued the poisonous serpent, Kaliya, in the polluted river Yamuna and danced on his hood, the rhythmic patterns emanating from the sounds of his feet gave rise to dance mnemonics.

While the *Natyashastra* mentions various gaits in Chapter xiii, the great Kathak patron, Nawab Wajid Ali Shah, has mentioned fourteen kinds of 'gats' in his works, *Saut-ul-mubarak* and *Gunchaye rang* and twenty-one kinds of 'gats' in another of his works entitled *Banni*. Thus, the entire gamut of the classified gaits in our treatises are not only employed in the portrayal of characters of the story enacted by the kathaks but the subtlety and beauty of each is presented in the traditional *gat nikas* format.

The seven classifications of gats in the *Sangeet Darpan* include

1) *Bhanavi* - (brilliant and blinding like the sun)
2) *Mainavi* - (frisky like the fish)
3) *Gajgamini* - (elephant)
4) *Turangini* - (horse)
5) *Hansini* - (swan-like)
6) *Khanjriti* - (sharp as the flashing sword)
7) *Mrigi* - (deer)

The *Abhinaya Darpan* has mentioned 10 categories of gaits.

athatra gati bhedanam lakshanam vakshyate kramat
hansi mayuri ca mrigi gajalila turangini
sinhi bhujangi manduki gatirvira ca manavi
dasaita gatayo gyeya natyasastra visaradaih

(namely, the ten gaits are the gaits of the swan, peacock, deer, elephant, horse, lion, serpent, frog, valourous and the maiden)

The *'gat nikas'* or introductory gaits, as the name itself suggests, is a unique instance of 'bhava-dikhana' (to show and establish emotions). Within Kathak alone, depiction of 'bhava' can be clearly demarcated within distinct aspects of 'bhava-dikhana' (to depict emotions), 'bhava-banana' or 'bhav batana' (to make emotions) and 'abhinaya' (emotion in mime). In the *gat nikas,* the static emotion of a state or an action is established; for example, the feeling or emotion behind the drawing of the veil across the face or the gait of an elephant or a horse, etc. is clearly being established by itself. This is quite distinct from the emotions being experienced and displayed while enacting a story using the veil or such gaits to denote either the beloved or the mother or a lady in the context of the action within the story.

The stories normally enacted are taken from the Puranas and Hindu mythologies. In former times, the gaits of the characters of a story in the 'gat-bhava' were first established throughout the 'gat nikas'. However, the horizon of the 'gat nikas' expanded to include many other gaits observed in nature, for example, the rowing of a boat, the strut of a peacock, the rolling of thunder and so on. The 'gat nikas' and the 'gat bhavas' are usually preceded by a 'palta' (to turn around) heralding a change within the story narration in a 'gat bhava'. Changes in mood and characters are also preceded by the 'palta'.

In the rendering of *abhinaya* (expression) in Kathak, the usage of neck, glances and moods lays emphasis on subtlety, spontaneity and naturalness. A mere flick of an eyebrow could denote annoyance or query while alternating upward movement of the eyebrows may denote the winding path taken by Lord Krishna. Thus 'bhava' (expression) to the text of the song can be rendered in Kathak through the (a) 'nayan bhava' through the media of eyes and pupil, (b) 'bol-bhava' symbolic interpretations, (c) 'artha-bhava' adhering faithfully to the literal meaning of the text, (d) 'nritya-bhava' using dance movements and patterns along with the interpretation, and (e) 'gat-artha-bhava' singing and emoting simultaneously. Thus, in these delineations, the Kathak makes maximum utilisation of the referential ('avidha'), metaphorical ('lakshana') and poetic ('vyanjana') interpretations of the text. To understand it further, 'darkness' can be interpreted in three different ways:

Avidha (direct, referential) - "*Darkness* sets in as soon as the sun sets."

Lakshana (metaphorical) - "We live in a *dark* age."

Vyanjana (poetic) - "Countless flowers float down the *darkness*."

As quite a few of the texts danced by the dancers revolve around 'sringar' (love), in the context of hero-heroine, the gods and goddesses being usually chosen for representation, the ten stages of love are:

'abhilasha' (longing), 'chinta' (anxiety), 'gunakirtana' (enumeration of the beloved's merits), 'anusmriti' (recollection), 'udvega' (distress), 'vilapa' (lamentation), 'unmada' (insanity), 'vyadhi' (sickness), 'jadata' (stupor) and 'marana' (death).

Again, in the delineation of 'bhava', it is important to assess the situation and state of the 'nayika' (heroine) and 'nayak' (hero). While the 'nayika', in terms of characterisation could be portrayed as the 'uttama' (dignified and refined), 'madhyama' (normal display of moods) and the 'adhama' (violent and unrefined, undignified display), the 'nayika' in love are eight and in terms of the age group are three states. The eight states of the maiden in love ('ashta-nayika') are:

Swadhinpatika	-	the maiden having her beloved in her grip.
Vasaksajja	-	the maiden in a state of readiness to receive her beloved.
Virahotkanthita	-	the maiden excited by separation.
Khandita	-	the jealous and aggrieved maiden.
Kalahantarita	-	the maiden who quarrels with her beloved and is then besieged by remorse.
Vipralabdha	-	the disappointed maiden whose beloved fails to appear at the tryst.
Proshitpatika	-	the pensive maiden separated from her beloved.
Abhisarika	-	the young maiden, blinded by love, goes in quest of the beloved or sends messages to him.

From the point of view of age, the three categories of 'nayaks' and 'nayikas' are 'mugdha' (the young maiden, ignorant of love), 'madhya' (the maiden confident of her youth and beauty) and the 'proudha' (the experienced and proud, self-assured maiden) while in terms of righteousness the three types of maidens include the *svakiya* (belonging to one), *parkiya* (belonging to another) and *samanya* or *ganika* (common or the courtesan respectively). In terms of gait and mood, the four categories of maiden are the *padmini* (beautiful and innocent with a sprightly lotus like gait), the *chitrani* (adolescent with a mature star-like gait), the *shankhini* (conch-like arrogance) and the *hathini* (elephant-gait, obese and filled with ire).

Similarly, in the characterisation of the heroes in love, the countenance and behavioural pattern dignified, not so dignified and totally undignified and uncouth (*uttama, madhyama* and *adhama*) are to be taken into account according to *karma* (deed). The hero is categorised as the *pati* (master, Lord), *uppati* (paramour) and *vaishik* (a person who associates with harlots). There are five further sub-categorisations of the *pati*:

Anukul	-	(friendly, kind, faithful)
Dakshin	-	(able, skilful, dexterous and competent; also sincere, honest and straightforward)
Dhrisht	-	(a faithless lover or husband; otherwise bold, confident bordering on rudeness and insolence)
Shath	-	(cheat, fraud, deceiver)
Anivigya	-	(ignorant, foolish)

The four 'abhinayas' (expressions) are applicable to Kathak. 'Angika' (body expression) is apparent because of the usage of every part of the body to enact the expression of the text or the rhythmic patterns; 'vacika' (speech) is employed while enacting the text. One special feature amongst the various possibilities of enactment is the poetry enacted to rhythmic recitation; 'aharya' is evident in the costume and make-up utilised within the dance form to highlight its salient features and 'sattvika' is the state of emotion that creates a sense of experience.

In Kathak as the name suggests, expression in story-telling is an essential feature which is rendered through various items such as the *gat-bhava, thumris, bhajans* and *dhrupad-dhamars,* etc.

In the *gat-bhava*, derived from *gati* (gait) and *bhava* (expression), through the medium of *mukha-abhinaya* (facial expression), *angabhinaya* (body expression) and *hastas* (hand gestures) only, not using any words, is a feature of *bhava-batana*. In this respect, it is akin to a pantomime, making full use of 'asamyukta' and 'samyukta' 'hastas'.

The usage of the *hastas,* according to their names, extends to the depiction of other movements and objects according to the text: two *katakamukha hastas* placed side by side, but facing opposite sides are used to denote the flute, symbolic of Lord Krishna, while a *kapittha hasta* with a *pataka* at its tail is used to denote a parrot.

The words 'hastas' and 'mudras' are usually used as synonyms; however, a 'mudra' by itself conveys a meaning unlike the 'hasta' which has to be seen in a context. But when able to communicate a meaning by itself, the 'hasta' is usually referred to as the 'hasta-mudra'.

The maximum use of the 'hastakas' or 'hastas' (both single hand and combined hand gestures) alongwith 'rasa-bhava' (emotions and moods with mime) making use of all the major and minor limbs of the body can be seen in the delineation of the 'gat bhava' wherein a whole story is told to the given metrical cycle (the 'lehera') which is given on the percussion and the stringed or musical instrument but without resorting to any text at all.

Evidence of 'hastakas' (hand gestures) arising out of a living dance tradition in the Gangetic belt can be seen in various treatises, other than the *Natyashastra*, such as the '*Hastakbhed*' written in Brijbhasha, the local dialect of central Uttar Pradesh, sometime in the late 12th Century or early 13th century and in the *Sri Hastamuktavali* authored by Shubhankar of Mithila (northern region of Bihar) in the 16th century, a treatise on hand gestures alone containing 955 slokas.

Quite a few regions in Bihar have strong leanings towards

Shaivism or the Shakti cult, despite a widespread Vaishnav atmosphere. It is this which is evident in the opening shloka of *Sri Hastamuktavali* where Gauri or Parvati and Shiva, in a romantic mood, discuss the meaning of two 'alapadma hastas' on the chest as well as of two 'kartarimukha hastas' placed together. The description encompasses 30 single hand gestures, 14 combined hand gestures and 27 dance gestures, thus enlarging the scope of gestures as given in the earlier works, like the *Natyashastra, Abhinaya Darpan, Sangeet Ratnakar*, etc., while also courageously differing with some points of view expressed in the *Natyashastra*. But much more revealing is the fact that the *Sri Hastamuktavali* gives a larger number of applications of the hastas as compared to the *Natyashastra* or the *Abhinaya Darpan*. For example, over 200 applications of *pataka hastas* are enumerated in the *Sri Hastamuktavali* as against 30, 41 and 21 of the *Natyashastra, Abhinaya Darpan* and *Sangeet Ratnakar* respectively. From a Kathak's point of view, what is important is that though some portions of the applications detailed in the *Natyashastra* and *Abhinaya Darpan* are applicable to all classical dance forms of India, yet in the extended application of the 'hastas' as detailed in the *Sri Hastamuktavali*, there are many such applications which find a direct applicability in Kathak.

The 'bhramara hasta' in *Sri Hastamuktavali* differs from that of the *Natyashastra, Abhinaya Darpan* and *Sangeet Ratnakar*. While in these three treatises, the forefinger is bent and the thumb and the middle finger are joined, the *Sri Hastamuktavali* describes the 'bhramara hasta' where only the middle finger and the thumb are joined, while the others are held up separately. A trembling 'bhramara hasta' thus is used to indicate a bee.

There are many such examples relating to the other 'hastas' of the *Sri Hastamuktavali* wherein a direct and clear application within Kathak can be seen.

Another peculiar feature of the dance form is the aspect of *bhava batana* (to tell *bhavas*) which is totally improvisatory in nature, wherein a line or word from the text is interpreted in a hundred different ways, depending upon the imagination of the dancer. Each interpretation of the line or word could be at a different plane namely from the mundane to the spiritual and the ethereal. To quote an example, *kaun gali gayo Sham?* (Which path was taken by my Shyam?). While 'Shyam' strictly means darkness, it is here a reference to Lord Krishna. In the interpretation, the 'gali' or path could be represented by the dancer as a normal path as is commonly understood or the dancer could take you through the path of the eye-kohl (referring to Shyam as darkness) or through the parting of the hair or through the rising smoke of a burning candle or through the dark veins of the body wherein runs the blood or the serpentine gait or the curvilinear long tresses or the by-passing of the dark cloud (Shyam) while the people wait eagerly for the onset of monsoon or the voyage through life to death (darkness).

Thus, in the delineation of 'abhinaya' especially the 'bhava batana', the Kathak unconsciously travels the entire gamut of 'alidha' (referential), 'lakshana' (metaphorical) and 'vyanjana' (poetic).

'Shringar' or romance through verses of 'thumris' centering on Lord Krishna and Radha saw new heights in their delineation. A subtle shift in emphasis changed the entire meaning and not mood of the sentiments expressed. For example, in the phrase

mohe chhedo mat jaayo nand ke chhail

(do not tease me; go away, son of Nand)

if the pause is placed after the word 'mat', Radha entreats Krishna not to tease her in various moods ranging from outright indignation to a lighter mood of refusal. However, if there is a shift in the pause and a break of breath is given after the word 'chhedo', then the entire meaning changes and now Radha prevents Krishna from going away as she would like to revel in more love-play.

The 'kavitt' derived from 'kavita' or poetry is rendered in two ways. While the meaning of the text in one exposition is rendered to the recitation of the text, in rhythm, rounding off to a rhythmic 'tihai' pattern, in the second exposition, it is rendered to the verses being sung without rhythmic accompaniment.

In the Lucknow 'gharana', it is felt that if a kavitt becomes a syllabic expression of a 'pada' or verse repeated on the drum syllables like dha, ge, na, etc. synchronising with the words of the song, then it would amount to reproducing the drum and the verse syllables by the feet which is considered disrespectful. However, in the Jaipur 'gharana', enactment of a kavitt to the recitation of the text is indicative of the vacikabhinaya of the Natyashastra. Keeping aside the differences between the two 'gharanas', the elements of bhava batana and abhinaya in the two expositions are brought out clearly. In the various mimetic expositions, the entire gamut of expression through the eyes (nayan bhava), through symbolic interpretations (bol bhava), through literal interpretation (artha bhava), using dance patterns (nritya bhava) and simultaneous vocal and mimetic rendering (gat artha bhava) are exploited. When the kavitt is interspersed with rhythmic patterns, then it is known as kavitt-paran.

A certain situation was posed as a question before the dancer who had to answer through the medium of poetry and dance; such a verse was known as prahelika. For example, an explanation is sought for the young bride's burnt hands, the answer could range from not knowing cooking to lighting a lamp, etc. Let us see what the Kathak said in his reply:

nai abala rasa reet na jaane, sej chaddhi jiya maahe dari,
rasa baat kahi, tab chonk pari, tab dahe ke kandhan baanh
dhari,
in dono ke jhakjhoran mein, katinar pitambar toot pari,
kar deepak se tan dhaank liyo, jin kaaran sunder haath
jali.

(The young bride sitting on the bed was absolutely naive
and hence was startled when he whispered words of love.
She struggled hard to get away from his arms but in
the ensuing struggle her clothes opened. She was
mortified and did not wish that anyone should witness
her plight. She therefore tried to put out the oil-lamp
which was the one and only witness and thus burnt her
palms)

After rendering the various mimetic aspects, the
complicated rhythmic patterns such as the 'pirmilu' and the
'parans' are danced, rounding off with spinning pirouettes at
a crescendo.

Paran means "crossing" in Sanskrit. Some scholars take
its root to 'prana' or decisive firmness. However, as far as
dance is concerned, it could also be a derivative of the word
'parinat' meaning 'the climax' which in execution, denotes
one of the finale rhythmic pieces danced by the dancer.
Some of the examples of 'paran' are 'jati paran', 'badhaiya ki
paran', 'yati paran', 'dopalli', 'tipalli', 'chaupalli', 'farmaishi'
and 'kamali' parans. When parans are associated with kavitt
(or recited poetry), it gives rise to 'kavitt-paran' such as the
'Ganesh paran', 'Shiva paran', 'ras paran', 'mahawat ki paran',
to name a few.

'Jati paran' is a paran based on one of the 'Jatis' viz.
'tisra', 'chatusra', 'khand', 'misra' or 'sankeema'. For example,
a tisra jati paran would indicate a pattern set to six beats or
its multiple in an interval of four beats.

'Badhaiya ki paran' is a set of rhythmic patterns with increasing pace of 'jatis' as well as expanding climax of each segment.

'Yati' indicates pattern of speech. Hence 'yati paran' is a rhythmic pattern set to varying speed. The 5 'yatis' are 'samayati', 'strotovaha', 'gopuchcha', 'mridanga' and 'pipilika'.

'Dopalli', 'tipalli' and 'chaupalli': As the names suggest, these are patterns which within one rhythmic sequence are done at two, three or four varying speeds or 'jatis' respectively.

'Farmaishi' and 'kamali parans': 'Farmaish' means a request and 'kamal' means something unique. Therefore, strictly speaking, a pattern presented on request is a 'farmaishi paran' whereas a pattern presented by the artiste highlighting its uniqueness is called a 'kamali paran'.

Similarly, 'pirmilu' is considered to be a derivative of 'para' + 'melu', i.e. the essence of a gathering (fair). In this case, the gathering is that of various syllables of percussion, dance, music and sounds of nature. Another interpretation is that of its being a derivative of 'parimal' or 'fragrance' of the various syllabi which form the rhythmic pattern. Both 'paran' and 'pirmilu' are rhythmic patterns of movements in Kathak. While 'paran' lays heavy emphasis on the syllables of the 'pakhawaj' (a long, base drum), the latter is embellished with syllables of all kinds of musical and percussion instruments. The finale usually consists of melodic-rhythmic pieces such as the 'tarana', 'sargam', 'chaturang', 'tirwat', 'adana', topped off by a fiery display of 'tatkar' (footwork).

According to the interpretation by the noted 'thumri' singer, the late Smt. Naina Devi, the exposition of Kathak denotes the cycle of life. The first signs of life: breath, the early stages of creation and childhood followed by adolescence wherein all possible emotions and fulfilments are witnessed and the last stage of destruction which is accompanied by a flurry of activity are convincingly portrayed through the *thaat, amad-toras-tukras, gat nikas-gat, bhavas - thumris - bhajans - kavitta - dhrupada - dhamars and paran - pirmilu - tatkar - chakkar* respectively. The tempo accordingly, moves from the slow to the sedate, from a medium pace to an intoxicating tempo, finally rising to a crescendo. The stage of crescendo wherein there is display of rhythmic patterns is really a higher state of involvement where words become meaningless and the dancer, the dance and the viewer have transcended the need for a text and share in that ultimate bliss.

On the anatomical plane, the devotional mind is akin to the 'ishtapada' ('vandana') whereas the initial introductory rhythmic patterns of 'uthaan' - 'amad' - 'thaat' are symbolic of the head ('moordhanga poornam'). The 'trotakam' consisting of 'toras - tukras' and the 'bhava - paragah' is symbolic of the bosom and the heart consisting of various 'gatis', 'bhavas', 'kavitts' and 'abhinaya' sequences respectively. Similarly, the 'parangah' encompassing 'parans-pirmilus' and the 'tatkar' is reminiscent of the fast pace of pulsating life of the lower body and the feet respectively while the 'tarana' is the ultimate sublimation of the entire persona.

The original Kathaks being themselves yogis or practitioners of yoga, automatically translated aspects of yoga into the dance form. Believing that the body has to be in a positive and receptive state as a prelude to sadhana and that the flesh. has then to be 'awakened' from dormancy, this can be achieved through a proper basic position of the dancer. It is believed that the body is made up of the five elements comprising of earth, water, fire, air and ether or space. The Kathak maintains his basic contact with the earth in the shortest linear route. According to the Lakshmi-tantra, with the place of the fire being at the heart and the breath being a vital point of contact between the self and the body so as to enable the vital airs of the body to purify the nerve circuits and impart vitality to the subtle centres of the body. The Kathak achieves this by maintaining contact at the heart with the two hands in an 'arala mudra'. Thus, the basic position of Kathak with the two hands in an inverted yogic position near the breast and the main axis of the body maintaining a vertical position, thus forms two triangles in the upper and lower parts of the body. The triangles as fertility symbols with the vertical axis denoting the gravitational pull. This symbolises the continuity of life and the resultant upward arrow is symbolic of the yearning of the soul for total surrender of the self. The union of the two triangles at the base leading to a circle also symbolises the union of Shiva and Shakti manifested in the creation of the universe. The three ends or corners of the triangle represent the three 'gunas' or principles of 'sattva' (equilibrium, truth and purity), 'rajas' (passion and great activity) and 'tamas' (emotional and mental darkness).

Similarly, the pose in which one hand is raised above the head while the other is stretched out stems from the basic role of the Kathak as the priest-storyteller who is the medium between the congregation and the Lord. In other words, the Kathak seems to say that 'whatever I receive from the Lord I pass on to the world'.

In the 'tatkar' derived from the words 'tallakari' or jhanatkari', various complicated rhythmic patterns and pieces are executed through the movement of the feet, making full use of the sole, heel and sides of the feet in a series of variegated patterns, at once bringing to the fore the dexterity in the usage of the feet and the permutations of a mathematical quiz. 'Tallakari' has been derived from the words 'talla' (sola of the feet) and 'kari' (activity) while 'jhanatkari' mentioned in the epic, Uttara Ramacharitamanas is also associated with the activity of the feet.

Manusmriti (the ancient book on Hindu codes) has mentioned the 'iiha' which means an exertion or an activity. A derivative of 'tri' (which stands for three) and 'iiha' (viz. an activity), the 'triha' was later corrupted to 'tihai' or 'tiya' which means 'thrice a certain activity'. This is used extensively in the dance form as a pattern being repeated thrice which forms the ending of a rhythmic pattern. This small rhythmic pattern is executed through movement of the feet and danced in between elongated patterns as punctuations.

The 'padhant' which means 'to read out' is a distinctive feature in any performance. In the execution of the rhythmic aspect of the dance the dancer, invariably, reads out the pattern of rhythmic syllables to be danced before executing the same. While this was born of a necessity to give syllables to the various sounds of nature and musical instruments to coordinated movements, it evolved into an art of recitation involving prolonged use of yoga especially the 'pranayama' aspect of breath controlling while uttering the complicated pattern between two energetic dance executions.

Rhythm in breathing is a balance among 'puraka' (inhalation), 'kumbhaka' (retention) and 'rechaka' (exhalation) which induces harmony within the inner elements. The controlled and meditative recitation of the rhythmic syllables involves the release and sucking in of breath which are closely related to the nature of the rhythmic syllables, reminiscent of the technique and approach to the chanting of tantric mantras which also lay great stress on breath control. As sound is conceived to be the specific quality of space, hence repetition of specific sound syllables create vibratory rhythms in the body which awaken the psychic fields. As an essential part of yoga and the tantric ritual, breath control through controlled emission of sound syllables are practised by the Kathaks themselves so as to stimulate the centre of paranormal consciousness in the brain centre for the arousal of the 'kundalini'. (The *kundalini* is the dormant psychic power lying coiled like a serpent at the base of the spine).

It is, therefore, no wonder that the tradition of the 'padhant' or recitation of the rhythmic mnemonics is reflective of the continuing tradition of the Kathaks of the temples of ancient India where enactment was preceded by recitation. *Padhant* also serves the purpose of acquainting the percussionist (who is a maestro in his own right and meets the dancer as accompanist on the stage itself, without prior rehearsals in the case of skilled and established dancers), with the mnemonics of the dance pattern to be danced. This practice, therefore, demands exactitude, precision and complete mastery and control over dance and 'layakari' (rhythmic tempo and pattern) on the part of the dancer so as to be able to match the alacrity and wit of the percussionist without losing control even for a split of a second while highlighting the scope for 'upaj' (improvisation). The mark of a good Kathak performer is the ease and fluidity with which the most difficult of rhythmic passages are uttered without making its intricacies hit the spectators visibly.

The ever familiar features of 'sawal-jawab' (question and answer) and the 'jugalbandi' (friendly competitions) between the dancer and the percussionist are appropriate examples of the innovative element in Kathak. Throughout the rendering of Kathak especially the rhythmic patterns, the rhythmic cycle is kept by the *lehera* on a musical instrument. To an undiscerning or an uninitiated audience, the *lehera* may seem a monotonous repetition of a musical cycle but this, however, forms the spine of the performance. Without the *lehera* marking time, it would be impossible to execute the various complicated rhythmic patterns as well as the *gat bhav* and the *gat nikas*. A dancer's mastery over rhythm is proved when the dance can be performed to the marking of the time cycle by the percussionist while the *lehera* continues simultaneously. This is, perhaps, the acid test for a dancer.

Thus, the relationship of Kathak and the *Natyashastra* is as thick and as close as it is in all the other dance and dramatic forms. The temple connection of Kathak was lost at some point of time in recent history and it became associated with the Mughal courts and the dance of the 'nautch' girls, emphasising the feudal attitude and approach to entertainment. However, the distinction between the true classical Kathak artistes in the court and the 'nautch' girls who were just common dancing girls was conveniently forgotten by various writers. In the process, they also overlooked an important factor of male artistes belonging to the Brahmin community, dancing in the courts of the nawabs. Interestingly, there was also a tendency to overlook the repertoire danced by all these traditional Kathaks which included pure rhythmic and mime sequences exhibiting the various moods and love-play of Radha and Krishna.

In this respect, special mention must be made of Thakur Prasad, Bindadin Maharaj, Achhan Maharaj, etc. of the legendary Lucknow school. The interest evinced by Nawab Wajid Ali Shah of Oudh (Avadh) and the patronage extended by him to music and dance have misled many to believe that Lucknow was the birthplace of Kathak. It was, perhaps, the association with the Mughal court which gave it a Mughal colour. The Hindu courts of Jodhpur, Jaipur, Raigarh, Benaras, etc. gave a lot of patronage to the Kathaks (again predominantly male artistes) which in turn gave rise to the Jaipur and Benaras schools of Kathak. Yet as Bindadin Maharaj stood out amongst the galaxy of artistes with his association with the Mughal court, this gave further credence to the Muslim court association of Kathak.

The census conducted by William Crooke, James Prinsep and Buchanan in selected areas of central Uttar Pradesh (around Benaras) and Bihar in 1891, 1825 and 1814 respectively, showing the presence of over 1300 Kathak establishments and categories of Kathaks practising in different regions, indicates that the art tradition was very old and therefore could not have been born in the 19th century in Lucknow.

Conforming with the Mughal court etiquette, the Kathak donned the 'churidar-angarkha' with the mandate to dance bare headed without the 'topi' (head gear) which was otherwise mandatory for all present in the court of the nawab. But the traditional 'lehenga-choli' (long skirt and blouse) continued to be worn in the Hindu courts. The 'churidar-angarkha' has also lent a lot of credence to the Muslim connection to Kathak. Here too, the short-lived memory of the populace comes into play, as this costume in its variations were not only in evidence in ancient India (Maurya and Gupta periods) but also were part of everyday costume of both Hindus and Muslims of certain regions (especially Punjab).

In the 50s, when there was a great spurt in cultural activities including innovations within Kathak in terms of duets, trios, dance-dramas, etc., in the true *Natyashastra* spirit of making the costume conform to the items, an item like the 'Mughal salami' (a purely rhythmic melodic piece) was danced with a costume which has been identified with the Muslim court over the ages. The hangover of 'salami' (Muslim way of greeting) continued for a long time in Kathak, whereas it had been discarded by the southern dance-forms danced in the court of the Nizam of Hyderabad.

But perhaps the maximum contribution to this false impression has come from the inaccurate depiction of Kathak in Hindi films.

As iconography was associated with Hindu temples and was, therefore, not given encouragement during the Muslim period, there are very few evidences of it in medieval India. Thus, a veritable treasure of possible reflection on the state of art in society was unavailable to the people of the area. The excavations of figurines of ancient India were small objects which were not immediately eye-catching as would be from a large temple.

Another combined reason could be the fact that as this age is closer to our times, it has been possible to unearth and ferret out names of skilled artistes who had left a mark.

Similar effort at tracing names beyond 200 years or so is proving a herculean task, because the earlier periods tended to anonymously emphasise the art rather than the artiste.

Another significant reason could be the use of local language and expressions rather than the elitist Sanskrit names (as used in the *Natyashastra*) and hence psychologically too, this tended to underplay the long traditional and rich history and legacy of Kathak.

To take a pirouette, it is usual to refer to it as 'taking the chakkar'. Incidentally, the category of 'chakra bhramari', 'to spin like a top', is to be witnessed only in Kathak amongst all the seven Indian classical dances.

Symbolism in Dance Poetics

The Kathak in his narration touches upon themes from Indian mythology. However, even atrocities committed by local rulers and landlords found their representations in various episodes of mythological tales wherein the 'devatas' (deities) fought the 'asuras' (demons); so did his love for God and mankind. But interestingly, consciously or unconsciously, the themes danced by him reflected the social attitudes and psyche, approach to nature and environment, philosophy of life as well as development of language.

The importance of the river to life is well evident in the deification of the rivers Ganga and Yamuna.

matah shailasutaspatnih vasudhahsingaraharvali
swargarohanavarjayanti bharantin bhagirathi prarthaye
twatire vasatwadambu pibatastvadwichishu prenkhat
stavanam smaratastwadarpitadrshah syanme sharirvyayah.

(garland of the earth, cohort of Parvati, let your pure water give sustenance to life and sanctify people.)

Similarly, the Yamuna has been addressed as the gracious benefactor who provides coolness from the heat and succour to the people in the following verse.

'kripaparavaram   tapantanayam   tapshamanim
murariprevaskan   bhavabhayadavam   bhakravardam
viyajjalanmuktam   shriyamapi   sukhapte   pratidinam
sadadhiro   nunam   bhajati   yamunam   nityaphaladam

(O' benevolent river, cooling the devotee from the heat of the sun; beloved of Krishna, benefactor of the people, harnessing the waters of the sky within her folds, providing succour to the people, we bow to you!)

The eternal desire within a young maiden to get a husband of her choice is well illustrated in the sequence of Parvati in meditation to win Shiva as her husband. Even in the *Ramcharitamanas*, the 'gauri pujan' describes Sita praying to Parvati to get the husband of her choice:

majjnu kari sar sakhin sameta gayee mudit man gauri niketa
puja kinhi adhik anuraga nij anuroop subhag varu maga

The 'swayamvara' system where the young maiden could indicate her choice seems to have been an established system in ancient India. Parvati wed Shiva despite formal objections by her father, Himraj. Similarly, the 'swayamvara' of Sita is well-known. But on the issue of chastity, polygamy and polyandry, all three seem to be norms of the ancient Indian society. Draupadi's wedding to the five Pandava brothers indicates the prevalence of polyandry while polygamy is evident in almost all stories of *Ramayana* and the

Mahabharata. King Dashratha had three wives while each of the five Pandava brothers had other wives besides Draupadi. The story of Dushyant and Shakuntala in Kalidasa's literary masterpiece *Abhijyan Shakuntalam* also is indicative of polygamy and sanctification of extra-marital relationships through the 'gandharva vivah' marriage before the Lord without the presence of other witnesses in terms of parents or society. Extra-marital affairs were permissible for men, and seems to have been permitted by society for women too as is borne out by the 'panchkanyas' (the five maidens); the rationale behind it according to one stream of thought, being that as each of the ladies concerned was with one man during a menstrual cycle and as each such a cycle is considered to be a purificatory process (or 'raktshuddhi'), they thus earned the status of 'panchkanyas' sanctified by society despite being 'bahubhogya' (married to many).

In a dichotomous situation, while polygamy and polyandry seem to be accepted in society, that very society sought chastity in a woman. Had it not been so, Sita would not have been made to go through the 'agnipariksha' (purification through fire). Angered by the insult heaped on husband Shiva by her father Daksha, Sati gave her life in the 'havan-agni' (sacrificial fire). The medieval period saw Padmini committing 'jauhar' in order to protect her honour and the honour of the Rajputs.

Sati is now a system of the past owing to the welcome social reformations wrought in the last 150 years.

The system of dowry which has become a curse for women in present-day India finds mention in *Ramayana:*

ath raja videhanam dadau kanyadhanam bahu,
gawan shatsahastrani bahuni mithileshwarah

(the Mithila ruler gave a lot in dowry including one lakh cows)

Lust for power, wealth and land rights was as relevant in our mythologies as it is today. Mahabharata is the story of a fight over landrights and hence for the throne between the Kauravas and the Pandavas while in Ramayana, Rama was exiled on the express wish of his stepmother, Kaikeyi, so as to make way for Bharata, her son, to rule over Ayodhya. Kansa was responsible for the death of many innocent children in order to protect his throne.

'Solah sringar' (or beautification) of the maidens has been an eternal subject for poets, sculptors and dancers. The heroine in various states of love, despair and hope form the subjects for dance and poetry. An overview of such poems of various periods brings out the attitude of society to inhibition. Kalidasa's description of the heroine in his works written around 400 AD focuses on an uninhibited description of the full youth of the maiden:

avarijita   kinchidivah   stanaabhyam   vaso   vasanam
tarunarkaragam
paryapt pushpastavakavanambra sancharini pallavini lateva

(wearing an apparel the colour of the rising sun and bent forward with her heavy breasts, her movements were like that of a creeper heavy with buds.)

Vidyapati, the celebrated Maithili poet of the late 14th to early 15th century, describes explicitly Radha confiding in her friend the love-play between her and Krishna as given in the following verse:

sunder kuchjug nakh khat bhari, jani gatj-kumbh bidaral
hari
adhar dasan dekhi jiyu mora kanpe, chand mandal jani
rahuk jhanpe

(my two breasts were torn with his nails as a lion teareth

the forehead of an elephant. When I see the marks of
biting on my lower lip, my heart trembleth as when
Rahu obscureth the circle of the moon)

Shortly, after the period of religious renaissance, there
appear many references to the veil. Romance was suggestive
and was personified by the shy glances of the eyes, quivering
lips and trembling hands and long tresses of hair in contrast
to the earlier explicit references to romantic fervour. Thus,
ghunghat ki gat (gait showing the drawing of a veil across
the face) and various kinds of glances through the diaphanous
veil became part of the Kathak repertoire.

a) *nain chahain mukh dekhiye, man sa kachhu durai,*
    man chahat drig moondi ke, lije hiye lagai
                                                (Rasleen)

(my eyes feast on the beauty of your face while my heart
embraces it with eyes closed)

b) *ghunghat ke pat khol re tohe piya milenge*
                                                (Kabir)

(draw the veil away from your face, for your beloved
stands before you.) Here, the beloved refers to God.

c) *mukhra dikha ja meri simtan pyari,*
    'akhtar' tum ghunghat to kholo
    payal bajaa ja meri dulhan pyari
                                    (Nawab Wajid Ali Shah)

(show your face, my love, remove the veil from your
face, let me hear the tinkle of your anklets)

d) *ye neechi nigahen, ye ada yaad rahegi*
    mil kar bhi na milne ki ada yaad rahegi

(I will always remember the subtle gesture of your lowered eyes as I will always remember our encounter)

Romantic desires and description of the body came to be expressed through the sinewy outlines of the heroine through her wet clothes in the late medieval periods as is seen in the following verse:

choonar mori bheej gayi 'Akhtar' jamuna beech

(Wajid Ali Shah)

(my veil will get wet on the beach of Yamuna)

This period also saw delicacy in romance through the touch of the wrist and the tinkling of the bangles.

Kanha mori bahiyan pakar leeni ho, ye dukh saho na jaaye, churiyan mori karki baaju lal bhaye, 'Akhtar' mohe haath na lagaye

(Wajid Ali Shah)

(Krishna caught my wrists and I can't bear the pain; my bangles have broken while my wrists have reddened, oh! do leave me to myself)

Even though the veil system seems to have become part of the social norm for ladies of medieval purdah in ancient India, yet the need for male protection comes through vividly in the various sonnets and verses of that period.

The association of glass bangles with marriage and widowhood came into vogue in medieval India. While green and red glass bangles became a symbol of a married woman, the breaking of glass bangles became synonymous with widowhood. Reference to glass bangles appear in Sanskrit literature only from the 11th century onwards.

Similarly, the practice of wearing nose-rings appears to have come into vogue in the medieval period, for neither the sculptures nor the literary works of ancient India (prior to eighth century AD) have any reference to the nose-ring which is quite surprising considering the extent of jewellery worn by the women of ancient India.

nath besar sira choti gundhai, bendi bhal sari pehnai
Binda kahat adbhut chhavi baniya re, dagar chalat...

(Krishna, adorned with nose-ring, plaits in the hair and in a sari is a beautiful sight to behold says Binda)

Another social factor which emerges in the various sonnets and poems is that of the man going away for long spells in order to earn his living, leaving his bride longing for his return. In many of these poems, there are references to her eagerly awaiting the return of her husband as spring draws near.

On the issue of child marriage, many verses have been enacted by the Kathaks. In the following verse, the bride laments the fact that her husband is still a child while she, though of the same age, has reached puberty and is desirous of fulfilment:

piya mor balak ham taruni, kaun tap chuklaun bhailon
janani,
pahir lel sakhi ek dachhinak chir, piya ke dekhat mor dagadh
sarir

(Vidyapati)

Even on the subject of morality the parameters and associated definitions change with time. For example, Kunti, the mother of the Pandavas, even after having conceived each of her sons from different Gods, is revered and treated with great respect, a situation very different from today's scenario. As regards drinks, verses from the ancient period refer to 'somras' as the drink or nectar of the deities, sanctifying the drinking of liquor. However, the morality of the medieval period took on a different connotation whereby liquor and intoxication became synonymous with eroticism and debauchery, the hangover of which continues till date.

On the religious plane, a sweeping view of the verses show a subtle emphasis on the various 'isms'. Ancient India seemed to adhere to a balanced worship of the various deities. The medieval period saw an inclination towards Vaishnavism in most areas of the Indo-Gangetic belt incorporating within its fold the essence of Sufism while Shaivism remained confined to small pockets of Rajasthan, Bihar, eastern Uttar Pradesh and Madhya Pradesh.

However, from the 12th-13th century onwards, development of modern dialects and regional languages following the 'Apabhransh' period is more clearly discernible leading to Urdu, Khari Hindi or Hindustani as we know them today and consequently its impact on dance-texts. At the same time, the importance of the local dialects and their influence on dance is also clearly visible as seen in the following verse:

a) *zehale miskin makun tagaful, doraye naina banaye batiyan*
ki tabe hijran na daram ai jan, na lehu kahe lagaye chhatiyan
shaban hijran daraz choon julf, va roze vasalat choon umra kotah
sakhi piya ko jo main na dekhoon, to kaise kaatoon andheri ratiyan

(Amir Khusro, 13th century)

(O' God, my beloved, do not be blind to my state, do not turn your eyes away with sweet words; I can't bear the separation so why don't you take me in your arms; your dark hair is like the despairing nights while your heart is young; if I am denied a glimpse of you, then how can I traverse the path of the dark nights?)

b) *adbhut gati upajat, ati nrittat, doyu mandal kunwar kishori*
sakal sugandh anga bhari bhori piya nrittat
muskan mukh mori, pari rambhan ras rori
(Swami Haridas, 15th-16th century)

(The beautiful gait, dance and fragrance of romance of the two beloved divine, gladden the heart)

c) *neend na parain raini jo awaan sej ke vaanchh janu koyi lawa*
dahe chand aru chandan cheeru, dagadh karai tan virah gambhiru
(Jayasi, 13th century)

(Comes nightfall but sleep has deserted me while I wait on the lonely bed; even the coolness of sandalwoodcannot cool the searing heat of my body)

d) *jab main tha tab hari nahi, ab hari hai main nahi*
prem gali ati sankari, ta main do na samahi
nainon ki hari kothari, putari palang bichhai
palkon ki chit dari ke, piya ko liya rijhai
(Kabir, 15th century)

(When Hari is there, I am not; when I am there, Hari is not; The lanes of love are so narrow that it cannot contain the two of us so I lure my beloved to the abode of my eyes and to the bed of my retinas covered with the sheet of my lashes)

e) *boojhat shyam kaun tu gori,*
   kahan rahat, kaki hai beti, dekhi nahin kahun brij khori
(Surdas, 16th century)

(Where do you stay; whose daughter are you? asks Shyam of Radha, for I've not seen you before!)

f) *dekhi siya sobha sukhu pawa, hriday sarahat bachanu na awa*
   janu biranchi sab nij nipunai, birachi bisva kaha pragati dekhai
(Goswami Tulsidas, 16th century)

(She saw him and he stole her heart; not a word could she utter as she stood transfixed)

l) *hori khelan ki san-san ghaten*
   aise khilari se dariye re
(Wajid Ali Shah, 18th century)

(He plays the colours of Holi with all; beware of such a bewitching player)

m) *sakhi ve mujhse kah kar jate*
(Maithili Sharan Gupta, 20th century)

(Friend, if only he had confided in me before going)

n) *chandni phaili gagan mein, chah man mein*
(Harivanshrai Bachchan, 20th century)

(Moonlight fills the sky while desire fills my heart)

The later part of the 20th century is concerned with the new idea of environment. Unconsciously, subconsciously or consciously, concern for the environment is discernible in various representations of the deities and in various episodes of our mythology. Each deity has been associated with a vehicle in the form of a bird or animal: Vishnu has been associated with the 'garuda' the bird, Shiva with Nandi the bull, Lakshmi with the owl, Durga with the lion, Kartikeya with the peacock, Yama with the buffalo, Saraswati with the swan, Ganesh with the mouse and Indra with the elephant. The snake is venerated as the 'naga' forming a garland around Shiva's neck and the 'anantnaga' or the many hooded serpent providing shade and the sleeping couch for Lord Vishnu. One of the popular stories relating to Shiva's snake garland is that during the churning of the ocean, in order to protect the deities, Shiva drank the poison of the King serpent Vasugi and, therefore, turned blue. But in order to cool his burning throat, he wrapped the cold-blooded serpent around his neck. This episode of Shiva gave him the title of 'neelakantha' (the blue-necked God) and draws attention to the importance of all sections of society including the cleanser of pollutants. Also, the mythological story relating to the birth of Ganesha, the elephant-headed God, is symbolic of the message to mankind to wield control over temper for as mortals, they are not vested with the divine powers of resurrection.

In another sequence from the Krishna legend, the killing or subjugation of the poisonous Kaliya, the serpent residing in the river Yamuna by Krishna is symbolic of cleansing the river of pollution. Similarly, the disrobing of Draupadi by Dushasana is symbolic of the disrobing the earth of its forest cover by modern man. This has been summed up in Dr. L.M. Singhvi's poem -

Dushasan bas karo, dharti ka cheer haran mat karo,
phir dwapar ko dohrane ka dussahas mat karo

(Dushasana, do not disrobe mother earth of her green cover!)

The 'govardhan' episode (lifting of the hill by Krishna on his little finger in order to protect the people from the torrential downpour) from the life of Lord Krishna as a result of the fury of Lord Indra and the final disappearance of Sita in the womb of the earth as given in *Ramayana*, are symbolic of the earth being prone to natural disasters like floods and earthquakes. The various poems, verses and sonnets in the context of the lover and the beloved give an idea of the various flora and fauna connected with the seasons and the geographical area of that region. Any mention of spring is usually accompanied with a description of the yellow blooming mustard fields and the sweet sound of the cuckoo while the monsoons refer to the fragrant smell of the earth and the dancing peacock while approaching winter is signified by falling leaves and cold wind. The verses also indicate the festivals associated with different seasons such as 'Holi' (festival of colours) with spring, 'Jhoola' (festival of swings) with monsoons and 'Diwali' (festival of lights) with autumn.

The lotus has been associated with divinity in Indian mythology as it is believed that the lotus is central to the 'kundalini' (potent occult energy) that is present. There are frequent references to the 'amla' (emblica officinalis or emblic myrobalan) which has been referred to as the fruit of the Goddess of prosperity. Similarly, various paintings and books refer to the 'neem' (azadirachta indica or margosa) tree as well as the 'jamun' (syzygium cumini) tree which signal the onset of summer. The 'jamun' tree has also been described in *Mahabharata* as a cosmic tree standing to the south of Mount Meru - the axis of the Universe. The 'tulsi' (ocimum sanctum or holy basil) has been referred in Hindu mythology as a holy shrub before which the King of Death (Yamaraj) gives himself away. The 'pipal' is considered sacred in the *Bhagvadagita* because of its association with light, the original sacred fire with which God granted knowledge to the human race and hence it is also known as the 'tree of life'. In a similar manner, verses and texts abound with visual and textual descriptions of various plants and trees such as the 'kadamb' (anthocephalus cadamba) around which Krishna sported with the 'gopis', the 'champa' (michelia champaca) which is considered as an incarnation of the Goddess of wealth, the jasmine or the 'mogra', the betel leaf or the 'paan', the 'dhatura' (datura alba or thorn apple), the 'amaltas' (cassio fistula or Indian laburnum) and the 'kachnar' (bauhinia variegata or bauhinia).

At a simplistic level, many symbolisms and parallelisms between rhythm in dance and the rhythm of nature could be drawn. The four major seasons, spring, summer, monsoon and winter could be likened to the four *matras* (beats) in each of the four divisions of *tritaal* (cycle of 16 beats). The waxing and waning phases and cycle of the moon, spanning 14 days and 28 days respectively, are reminiscent of the cycle of 7 and 14 beats, the 12 months in a year, symbolic of the 12 beats of *ektal* and *chautal* are beautifully represented in the *barahmasa*, the folk song of eastern UP and Bihar. The 'cakra-bhramari' executed by the Kathaks are reminiscent of the rotation of the earth around its axis as well as the orbiting of the planets.

Even on the scientific front it is interesting to see the seeds of present-day technology and concern in our mythologies. The 'pushpa-viman' used by Ravana to abduct Sita can be taken as a precursor of the modern aeroplane. The Jambuvan doctor and the requirement of 'sanjivini booti' is a pointer to natural herbs and herbal medicine. The episode of Durga trying to kill the demon war-general, Raktabeej, and the emergence of multiple Raktabeejs with every drop of blood is reminiscent of atomic fission.

The birth of Karna from *Surya* (sun or energy) can be likened to a birth through artificial insemination. The *astra-shastra* (weapons) used in the various episodes of our myths clearly reflect bio-chemical warfare. At the same time it would be worthwhile to dwell on the cautionary note given by Narad to Arjun in *Mahabharata* for not using specific kinds of *astra-shastra* till absolutely necessary as it would be harmful to ecology. This note of caution is equally relevant today. The building of the *setubandh* (bridge) by Hanuman and his group is clearly an indicator towards knowledge of bridge technology.

Thus, throughout the known history of dance in the last 2500 years in the region there is a clear influence of the philosophy, social attitudes, and customs of the age. One constant factor which emerges in the entire span of the ancient, medieval and modern India is the emphasis given to human values, human ethics and the spirit of sacrifice and tolerance as subsequently there is always the depiction of good winning over the forces of evil.

Dance and Music

'Katha kahe so Kathak kahlaye. . . .' While talking of
theme, poetry and music in Kathak, nothing could be more
apt than this phrase. As is evident from its origin, a group
of traditional story-tellers who retold tales from mythologies
and epics through the medium of dance and music, the
poetics in Kathak, traditionally, formed the central pillar of
the dance. Moved by natural beauty and an instinctive urge
to pay reverence to the Maker the Kathaks communicated
this joy through their dance. However, in a gradual
conscious development, it took the form of an art. Thus,
the narrator became the dancer. Being located traditionally
within the thresholds of the temples, addressing the
congregation gathered within the premises, he danced to
Rigavedic shlokas in praise of the deity by enacting the
mythological tales connected with Him. Not only did he
dance to stories of the Lord but also local legends,
'prabandhs' and 'kirtanas'.

The word 'prabandh' comes from the root *'pra + bandh'* which means "to tie down firmly" and, therefore, in literary parlance, it is used to denote a composition or a continued narration. The various compositions to which the dancer danced included the *slokaprabandh* (verse), *kavya-prabandh* (epic) or *geet-prabandh* (song). The language employed, apart from the elitist Sanskrit, was the dialect of the area in order to reach out to the people. Throughout history, Sanskrit remained the language of the court and the elite while Prakrit and Pali formed the lingua franca of the people. It is, therefore, not surprising to find Emperor Ashoka of the Mauryan dynasty setting up his edicts not in Sanskrit, but in the languages spoken and understood by the general masses.

With the formal writing of the epics, *Ramayan, Mahabharat* the various Puranas and other great literary works, these were also included in the Kathak repertoire. No verse, story or poetry which lent itself to dramatic and emotional appeal revolving on subjects closely affecting the lives of the people could be left aside. The accompanying music was influenced in the earlier periods by the limited number of musical notes relating to the Vedic chant which gradually gave way to musical compositions with the inclusion of syllables and notes as the system of ragas came to stay.

With the 'dhrupad' and 'dhamar', the literary and musical content of Kathak depended heavily on these compositions. 'Dhrupad' has been derived from 'dhruva-pada' which means a firm step and was essentially religious, sombre and grave in nature. The compositions of 'dhrupad' and 'dhamar' based itself on hymns in praise of the Lord while also, narrating, at times, a sequential event. The meaning of the words of the composition were rendered by the Kathaks through the media of 'mukha-abhinaya' (facial expression and body emotions) and by extensive use of transitory emotions.

The decay of Hinduism, the establishment of Muslim rule in India and the consequent Bhakti Movement (religious renaissance) marked the beginning of a different epoch in the annals of the Kathak tradition. Not only did the period witness a literary and musical renaissance but also experienced the blossoming of the Ras-leela tradition and the predominance of the bhakti (devotional) tradition in Kathak along with a paradoxical blooming of the virtuous aspect of the dance form. The poetry of Swami Haridas, Namdev, Meera, Kabir, Vidyapati, the Ashtachhap poets Surdas, Nanddas, Parmanand, Kumbhadas, Krishnadas, Chaturbhujdas, Govindaswami and Chittaswami became deeply entrenched in Kathak and the Ras-leela traditions whereby the dancers emoted the verses of the great poets, saints and mystics. Poets of the Bhakti Movement belonged to all castes and their lyrics and verses in the local dialect were short, intense and precise.

The development of the various technical limbs of the dance also showed a parallel growth with the development of the classical music tradition in the area. The 'khayal' which gained ground in the medieval period and included attractive features found echoes within the dance form.

While it is usually suggested that the word 'khayal' has a Persian origin yet the word 'khela-pada' which means *a sportive step* finds mention in Kalidas's *Vikramorvasiya* (Act IV, sloka XIV), where the 'khelapada' has been used to describe the gait of Urvashi when compared to that of a swan. Thus, it is quite likely that the word 'khayal' is a derivative of 'khela-pada' just as 'dhrupad' is a derivative of 'dhruva-pada' as both these terms relate to gaits, the former being sportive, playful and amorous while the latter is formal and dignified. The same ethos prevails within the virtuous and technical aspects of the Kathak form vis-a-vis the emotive aspect. Incidentally, Shri Chaitanya Desai derives the word 'khayal' from the Sanskrit word 'khela' which stands for 'a dramatic performance' while in the Rajasthani dialect, 'khela' means the 'performance of a folk play'.

An incident has been narrated by Shri L.D. Joshi, the noted khayal singer of the 19th century, wherein Miyan Haddu Khan sang a khayal set to *ektal* (a cycle of twelve beats) in slow tempo executing only the *gamak-tans* to which the audience of Calcutta, attuned to dhrupad music, reacted favourably as compared to the khayal sung at medium tempo with all the embellishment of *murki, harkat, tan,* etc. This was indicative of the proximity of khayal to the dhrupad style even as late as the 19th century.

Another significant arm in the repertoire of Kathak is the 'thumri'. While it is commonly believed that the word 'thumri' is derived from 'thumak' which means to 'walk in a sprightly and rhythmic manner' and 'rijhana' namely 'to please', yet the *Sangeet Damodara* (15th century) mentions the composition 'jhumri' (an intoxicating step).

It is also interpreted that from the Kauthum branch of singers and dancers, mentioned in the Samaveda and the sage Tumbaru, an adept dancer, whereby the mimetic aspects of the dance came to be known as 'tumbaru', later distorted to 'thumri'. Sage Tumbaru has been mentioned in the *Sangeet Ratnakar* of Sharangdeva.

The *Sangeet Damodar* also defines 'sangeetaka', derivative of the 'sangai' (to sing together) as

talavadyanugam gitam natibhiryattu giyate
nrityasyanugatam sange tat sangeetakamuioyate

(Sangeetaka is a song presented on the stage by a dancer to the accompaniment of rhythm, instruments and dance)

It has, therefore, been derived by Shri M.V. Dhond, a musicologist, that while 'dhrupad' was a 'tandava' or a virle dance form, the 'thumri' was a 'lasya' dance.

As the 'thumri' or 'jhumri' means an intoxicated step (again a reference to gait), it embodies within itself the feelings and tender emotions experienced by men and women.

In the Indus-Gangetic belt, it was a usual feature for the
man to go away on work from his native place leaving behind
his young wife in full bloom. Many songs have been written
about the onset of spring, with tender young buds, rows
and rows of mustard in the fields, the fresh nip in the air
awakening similar languorous emotions within the young wife
waiting for fulfilment with the return of her husband:

aaya basant chalat poorvayee
chhaye phoolanawa sarson leharaye
bole koyaliya kunjan kunjan
dole bhavara galiyan galiyan
nachat gawat khelat sung sub
rang rachawat dhoom machawat
kinh sung nachat ras machayai
aas lagayai chain churayai
katat nahi mohe sooni ratiyan
kabahun awahain meet piyarawa

(spring is here with its cool breeze and swaying mustard
fields; cuckoos sing in every bough, bees buzz all around;
dance, music and colour rend the air; but with whom
should I dance for I desire the return of my beloved; he
who has stolen sleep from my eyes and peace from my
heart)

Many songs have been written about the onset of the
monsoon, the rolling thunder, the pitter-patter of rainfall,
the fresh smell of the earth, the dance of the peacocks and
the young beloved sending messages to her husband via the
dark clouds to return home:

gheri gheri aayee kari badara
barsela boondan boondan phooharava
dekhat nachela ban ban morva
aumi sugandh chahun or hariyali

aise mein hum baithee akeli
tarpat tarpat tarasat jiyara
sajan mor kahan kit jayoon
lekar sandeswa ja re badariya...

(The sky is overcast with dark clouds; in the falling rain, the peacocks dance; sweet smell of the earth fills the air; but I sit alone, anxious to be united with my beloved; O! clouds, take my message to my loved one!)

The familiar pining of Radha and the gopies for Lord Krishna and their emotion evoking love play and their overflowing joy at the sight of his are expressed vividly through the medium of 'thumri' where emotions play a dominant role:

batade sakhi, kauna gali gaye Shyam
gokul dhundi, Brindaban dhundi
dhunda phire chari dhama
raina divasa mohi tarapata biti
bisara gaye saba kama

(O! friend, show me the lane by which Shyam went; I have combed the whole of Gokul and Brindaban. I have sought him in all the four sacred places; I have been restless day and night, neglecting all the work)

The rise of Vaishnavism with Lord Krishna as its central theme was beautifully described and rendered through the medium of 'thumri'. This was vividly exploited by the Kathaks.

With the introduction of Urdu poetry, namely ghazal, to the music repertoire of the singers, a parallel influence was seen in the dance repertoire. In emoting the meanings of the text, the Kathak gave two simultaneous interpretations to it: one that of the emotions between the lover and the beloved and the other in terms of this divine love and the yearning for God.

Natural sound is an integral part of body language. The much awaited cry of a new-born baby transmits certain definite signals to the hearer. Expression of pain and joy are manifest in the positioning of the body accompanied by a throaty sound. Thus, the earliest inflections of speech, cries of grief, pleasure and desire led to the development of music with pitch and tonal differences. According to the Patanjal theory, the internal heat of the body plays an important part in the production of the sound of the voice. When the soul wishes to speak, the mind acts upon the abdominal fire which sends a signal to the vital air pervading the ligament below the navel (*brahma granthi*) thereby causing the *ati sukshma nad* or the very intense sound in the region of the abdomen, the *sukshma nad* or the minute sound in the chest, the *pushta* or the developed sound in the throat, the *apushta* or suppressed sound in the mind and the *kritrima* or artificial sound in the mouth. The strength of the initial force dictates the primary movement of air. Based upon these chords are the 22 *srutis* or particles of sound which are the essential features of the Indian *saptaka* or the heptachord.

The accompanying music to Kathak is the Hindustani classical music based on the system of ragas. While the Vedic chant ranged around three basic notes, human emotions, local folk songs, songs of ascetics and the various surrounding influences of nature led to a range of haunting melodies with a sense of rhythm and emotional appeal (covering the twelve note format of C, D, E, F, G, A and B, B flat, A flat, F sharp, E flat and D flat). This gave birth to the system of ragas. The raga which literally means colouring in Sanskrit is a melodic scheme built on the permutation-combination of the seven basic notes and the five supplementary notes. It, therefore, indicates colour imparted to the inner subconscious of man affecting his mood. In its delineation, it is a composition in space.

The musical forms within the raga system are broadly categorised as the *anibaddha*, not bound and seemingly free of rhythmic discipline and the *nibaddha* or bound. In Kathak, it is the *nibaddha* aspect which is normally used especially while emoting or dancing to a verse, *prabandh, bhajan, thumri, tarana, tirwat* or the keeping of the time cycle with the *lehra*. The usage of the *anibaddha* which also exists is, however, limited. One of the important examples of the *anibaddha* is the dancing to a *kavitt* as delineated by dancers of the Lucknow 'gharana' (school) of Kathak. Within the Bhatkhande school of music, the ragas, according to the mood they evoke and their characteristics, have been classified under ten major *thaats* or *melas*, each consisting of a set of seven *swaras* (musical notes) which are:

1) Bhairav (Sa ri Ga Ma Pa dha Ni, C Db E F G Ab B)
2) Bhairavi (Sa ri ga Ma Pa dha ni, C Db Eb F G Ab Bb)
3) Asavari (Sa Ri ga Ma Pa dha ni, C D Eb F G Ab Bb)
4) Bilawal (Sa Ri Ga Ma Pa Dha Ni, C D E F G A B)
5) Todi   (Sa ri ga ma Pa dha Ni, C Db Eb F# G Ab B)
6) Kalyan (Sa Ri Ga ma Pa Dha Ni, C D E F# G A B)
7) Kafi   (Sa Ri ga Ma Pa Dha ni, C D Eb F G A Bb)
8) Khamaj (Sa Ri Ga Ma Pa Dha ni, C D E F G A Bb)
9) Marwa   (Sa ri Ga ma Pa Dha Ni, C Db E F# G A B)
10) Poorvi (Sa ri Ga ma Pa dha Ni, C D E F# G Ab B)

From these stream the entire possible range of ragas and raginis. Of these the major melodic disciplines were called ragas owing to the masculine appeal they evoked. The melodic disciplines, soft, evocative and feminine in nature, were dubbed raginis. A personification of the mood and rasa evoked by the ragas-raginis (melodic disciplines) can be witnessed in the Ragamala paintings of the 16th century to the 18th century.

For instance, Raga Malkauns has been depicted as a hero wearing a blue robe with a string of pearls on his shoulders, holding a staff in his hand and accompanied by lady attendants. 'Dressed in blue, his shining complexion puts to shame the prince of Kaushaka. With garlands on his shoulders and a white staff in hand, he is the very picture of the purity of the flavour of love. He overpowers the hearts of women and by his beauty attracts the gaze of all'. Ragini Todi is taken to be the beloved of Raga Malkauns and is represented by a beautiful maiden dressed in white.

Besides the masculine and feminine emotions evoked by the ragas-raginis, they are closely intertwined with the time cycle—be it the planetary motion bringing with it the various seasons or the time cycle of a day. The life cycle of the basic seven notes of an octave has been described by Mr. Awasthy of Kanpur as follows:

Sa (i.e. Do) - the *silanad* of Brahma: breath, the first sign of life.
Re (i.e. Re) - *Riturishabh*: *vasana* followed by *upasana bhava* or awareness of life around.
Ga (i.e. Mi) - 'gati' (gait) as in adolescence.
Ma (i.e. Fa) - 'manan' (maturity).
Pa (i.e. So) - 'parityaga' (spirit of sacrifice and adjustments).
Dha (i.e. La) - 'dhyana' (meditative).
Ni (i.e. Ti) - 'namana' (final surrender to the Almighty).

Drawing inspiration from nature, Abul Fazl has recorded the origin of each note of an octave in the following manner:

Sa   (shadaja)   -   peacock
Re   (rishabha)   -   *papiha* (bird - call)
Ga   (gandhara)   -   goat
Ma   (madhyama)   -   crane

Pa   (panchama)   -   *koyal* (bird - call)
Dha   (dhaivata)   -   frog
Ni   (nishada)   -   elephant

Thus, Raga Basant and Raga Bahaar bring to mind the nostalgia of spring and the freshness of nature after the cold winter and Raga Malhar is reminiscent of the pitter-patter of the falling raindrops and the smell of the earth. On a micro-scale, Raga Bhairavi is sombre, serene and graceful in mood, evoking the devotion and calm of morning while Raga Pooriya, Sri Raga and Raga Darbari are evocative of twilight and the late evening mood. According to some, the six principal classifications of Ragas are Hindol producing the sweetness of spring and exuding the fragrance of flowers, so evocative of serenity and calm filling the mind with gladness, Megh reproducing the humidity of the clouds and rain, Deepak with its ability to kindle a fire, Bhairav carrying the freshness of dawn and the song of the early birds and Malkauns producing sweetness and relaxation in the mind. Sharangadeva, in his *Sangeet Ratnakar*, mentions the existence of over 664 ragas and raginis.

It is believed that Indian music possesses great phychological and elemental power and, therefore, the vibrations emanating from the execution of a raga can not only cure certain ailments but also cause events appropriate to its mood. It is popularly believed that Tansen (whose original name was Tanna Misra), son of Makarand Pande, a Hindu priest of Gwalior, who later became one of the greatest singers the country has ever known and who lived during the reign of Akbar the Great, kindled a fire by the sheer power of his rendering of *Raga Deepak* which could only be extinguished by the equally powerful singing of *Raga Megh Malhar* which effected a downpour.

While rendering Kathak dance, care is taken to use suitable ragas appropriate to the time of the performance in the *ehera* (keeping of time-cycle). As regards the *abhinaya* (expressional, mimetic) aspect, appropriate ragas are used for the different characters, time, circumstances and mood contained in the text which is being enacted in dance. Thus, in any mime composition, *abhinaya*, relating to spring would be rendered with appropriate movements and *bhava* (mood) in *Raga Basant* or *Raga Bahaar*. While rendering a *thumri*, even with the presence of a predominant raga, the music could take beautiful, languorous diversions so as to evoke the mood suitable for not only *sanchari bhavas* (transient moods) but also for *bhav banana* and *bol bhava* wherein as many interpretations to the text is manifested as possible.

Music and rhythm are the two important limbs of dance. Had it not been for the orderly rhythmic movement of the planets, there would be chaos in the universe. The timely sequence of the different seasons and of the daily movement of the sun bringing about day and night, and the waning and waxing phases of the moon are indications of the importance of rhythm. *Tala* has been defined in the *Amarkosh* as a measurement of time. In the *Sangeet Ratnakar*, Sharangadeva has written:

talastalapratishthayamati dhayorghana smritah
gitam vadyam tatha nrityam yatastale pratishthitam

(experts dwell on the importance of tala, rhythm, as it is closely linked with vocal and instrumental music and dance)

The word *tala* has been derived from the Sanskrit word *tal*, (palms of the hand which are used to strike each other in order to produce a beat). Mythologically, it is believed that *tala* is comprised of 'ta' + 'la', 'ta' being taken from the *tandava* (virile) dance of Shiva and 'la' from the *lasya* (graceful) dance of his consort Parvati.

Evolving from this, in order to have a fixed measure of time enabling dance and music, the tala system contains a definite cycle of beats (*matras*) and maintenance of speed (*laya*).

The even tempo being the simplest of rhythms saw the fixation of one of the most widely used *talas* : *trital* (or *teental*, i.e. a cycle of sixteen beats). The cycle is called an *avartan* or *avardi*.

Similarly, all other well-known talas are multiples of two, three, five, seven, nine, eleven, thirteen, etc. There are many talas which are not whole numbers, such as cycles of five-and-half, nine-and-half, etc. The *Sangeet Ratnakar* mentions the existence of 120 talas while Dulha Khan in his *Swar Sagar* has stated that even though there are over 5900 talas, yet there only about sixteen which are in popular use.

As in music, even the talas evoke its characteristic mood and rasa. For example, *teental* or *trital* is romantic, serene and wholesome, while *dhamar* is grave and sombre. Similarly, the *chautal* is deep and dense while *ektal* is light-hearted, even though both denote cycles of twelve beats. Thus, while performing Kathak the dancer has to pay particular attention to the right usage of the tala according to the text.

If the tempo or speed (laya) of the same tala is doubled, two cycles are completed within sixteen beats, then the total number of beats covered is thirty-two. This tempo is known as the *madhya laya* vis-a-vis the *vilambit laya* or slow tempo. Similarly, if four cycles are covered within sixteen beats, thereby executing sixty-four beats, the tempo thus attained is the *drut laya* or fast tempo. A tempo much slower than the slow *vilambit* is the *ati vilambit* and the tempo much faster than the fast drut is the *ati drut*.

While rendering the various *jatis* (classifications of tempo) used within the Kathak form include the *treyashra* or *tisra* (three beats to be interpolated in each interval of a tala), *chatushra* (four beats within the interval), *khand* (five beats within the interval), *mishra* (seven beats within the interval) and *sankeerna* (nine beats within the interval). Similarly, extensive use is also made of the *adilaya* or *arilaya* (six beats juxtaposed against four beats), *kuadi laya* (five beats juxtaposed against four beats) and the *viadi laya* (seven beats juxtaposed against four beats). However, the *sahitya* or text is generally not danced to various *jatis* and *laya* but relates itself to a particular *laya* and *jati*. Care has to be taken while choreographing a particular text.

Similar sentiments have been expressed by the Karnat ruler Nanyadev of Mithila (11th century) in the treatise *Saraswati Haridayalankar* popularly called Bharatbhashya as

kiyanto niyata ragalyeshu pratipadita rasanuradhadanyepi ragah karya maneeshibhi

(the medium tempo should be used for moods of mirth and love, slow tempo for the mood of sadness and fast tempo for moods of valour, anger, disgust and fear. Thus, musical compositions for dance depend on the metre of the verse, mood of the text, location and circumstances described within the text thereby imparting to it emotional, ethical, cosmic and philosophical connotations.)

In a usual rendering of the rhythmic patterns, the Kathak dancer would begin the pattern on the *sama* or beat 'one' of the cycle and after traversing through the number of cycles required according to the pattern, end with a flourish on beat 'one'. The four ways in which the rhythmic patterns *toras-tukras*, *parans-pirmilus*, etc. could begin and end, as danced in Kathak are the *sama*, *atit*, *anaghat* and *visham*.

samatitanagatashcha vishamashcha grahamatah chatvarah kathitastale sukshmadrishtaya vichakshanai

(the four grahas in talas are sama, atit, anaghat and visham)

In the '*sama-graha*', the rhythmic patterns while starting in the *sama* i.e. beat 'one' of the cycle, also ends on the *sama*. In the '*atit*', the pattern finishes on a beat after the sama while in the 'anaghat' and 'visham', it finishes on the beat before the sama and on the third division respectively.

The rhythmic patterns have various flavours, such as the *sangeet ka tukra* and the *gopuchcha*. In the former, musical syllables and rhythmic mnemonics combine to form a pattern which is danced while in the latter, like a cow's tail (as the name suggests) the rhythmic pattern tapers off to a close. Others include the *samayati* (where the pattern maintains the same tempo throughout), the *strotovaha* (where the pattern starts at a slow tempo and ends at a fast tempo) resembling the course of a river from a trickle to a water-fall and to its meeting in the sea, *mridanga* (where the pattern starts and ends at a fast tempo and has a body with a slow tempo) and *pipilika* (where the pattern starts and ends at a slow tempo with the body being performed to a fast tempo).

Items with rhythmic musical compositions include the *tarana*, *adana*, *tirwat* and *chaturang*. The *tarana* and *adana* are musical compositions set to a particular *raga* and *tala*. The *tirwat* is a musical composition based on rhythmic syllables predominantly of *pakhawaj* and dance while the *chaturang* has four distinct divisions, each division separately emphasising the words of the song, syllables of a *tarana*, syllables of a *sargam* (musical notes) and mnemonics of a pakhawaj.

The *sargam* (musical piece based on the notations of a raga), *tirwat* (rhythmical musical piece based on the musical syllables along with dance mnemonics) and the *tarana* (lyrical pattern based predominantly on musical syllables) which were offshoots of the *khayal*, were also incorporated within the repertoire. The last few centuries also showed a spurt of literature based on the theme of Krishna and Radha. Just like Hinduism which incorporated within its fold various nuances, the dance form also incorporated phrases of contemporary poetry written in Brajbhasha, Hindi, Rajasthani, Bhojpuri, Avadhi, Maithili and Urdu.

Costumes and Instruments

The beauty of the human form has captured the imagination of sculptors in all ages. Hence the attempt of the artiste has frequently been to depict the yakshas, yakshis, salabhanjikas and the dancing scenes with the barest minimum of clothes, in order to accentuate the rhythmic grace of the human body. Nevertheless, the sculptures available from the Indus-Gangetic region provide an insight into the development of costumes and musical instruments both of which are extremely essential to the performing arts. What is striking is their deep relation to the lives and habits of the lay person.

Earlier, three major classifications of *abhinaya* had been given. A fourth could be added: '*aharyabhinaya*' in terms of make-up and costume. The link between the four abhinayas has been summed up by Bharata in his *Natyashastra* as:

Vayunurupah, prathamasthu, veeshah
veeshanurupina gatipracharah

gatipracharanugatam ca pathyam
pathyanurapah abhinayascha karyah

(make-up and costumes should be in accordance with the age and nature of the characters, followed by proper movements and gestures, correct enunciations and finally by responsive emotional reactions)

While discussing the costume of a Kathak dancer, the question about stitched clothes needs to be discussed. It is usually believed that sewn clothes came into vogue during the medieval period of Indian history; however, a study of Vedic literature provides reference to the knowledge of the art of sewing in *Rigaveda*. The following verse

seevyatvapah soochya achhidyamanaya

mentions the needle for stitching together two pieces while the next verse from Aitareya Brahmana (II.32.4) clearly mentions two pieces of cloth being joined together by a needle.

yatha soochya vasah sandagheeyat
evamevaitabhiryagyasyachhidram sandaghet

The tailor has been mentioned in the *Amarkosha*. The observations of Itsing, the Chinese traveller, indicates the popularity of shirts and trousers in the seven century AD in Kashmir and Punjab. The Buddh and Jain clothing for the nuns permitted *samghati* for the lower part, *antarvasaka* for the upper part and *uttarsang* as a covering garment. The young nuns could also wear *kanchuki* (a kind of bodice).

As the Gangetic belt was in contact with the western world, the Greeks, the Scythians and the Persians, this facilitated the spread of the fashion of stitched clothes.

However, as society seemed to have a favourable inclination towards the indigenous clothing which was more suitable in terms of weather, stitched clothes (trousers and frock or shirt) were adopted visibly by dancers of various eras of ancient India (e.g. Nati of Patliputra and dance panels of

Didarganj Yakshi from third century BC.

Representation of Tara from Monghyr; tenth century.

Deoghar and Sanchi) in addition to the local dressing habits. Even during the medieval period of Indian history when the Mughal empire held sway, the elitist Sanskrit of earlier times was replaced by the elitist Farsi but once again churidar-kurta came to be increasingly associated with the royal way of dressing and the apparel of choice of the dancers in the Muslim courts.

In terms of sculptures, what emerges is the accent on the beauty of the human form which was to be covered only minimally with clothes. Thus, the torso was covered with a loose cloth with pleats so as to give the necessary walking space, while the breasts were left bare—to be covered by heavy chunks of jewellery.

(This is still in vogue in the Santhal Paraganas, Chhota Nagpur and the tribal belts of Bihar, Madhya Pradesh, parts of North-eastern India and Malabar. It is not so common in the north and north-west regions of the country in deference to the harshness of the cold weather).

This, therefore, laid the foundations of the *sari* and the later *lehenga* and *lungi* from the *vikachchha* form when the drape did not pass between the legs for being tucked at the back. When the end was passed between the legs and tucked at the back, this gave rise to the *sakachchha sari* and the *dhoti*. Interestingly, all the terracotta statues of dancing girls and the Didarganj Yakshi of Patliputra from the third century B.C. relating to the Mauryan period, the stone and bronze sculptures of the Gangetic belt belonging to the Saka, Gupta and the Pala periods are evidence of the *vikachchha* while the Gandhara *ignai* statue (in human form) of second century AD is a pointer towards the *sakachchha* way of wearing the sari. There is a striking similarity to the dress worn by the Egyptian lady where the drapes of the dress and over the arm is suggestive of a *vikachchha sari*.

The sculptures of Bharhut and the Sanchi panels reveal the wrapping of a long piece of cloth around the waist, pleated at the centre to enable movement of the legs and tucked between the legs to be looped backwards giving rise to the dhoti system. The dhoti ended often either above the knees or slightly below the knees as seen in the dance panels from Bharhut and some of the figures on the Mathura railings.

The upper part of the body was for the most part bare, covered only by heavy jewellery. The head often sported a

The figure of Ushebti from Egypt.

head gear. However, the yakshi holding the portals of the
gate and the yakshi with the *baddha cari* position in Sanchi,
including the figures of the couple from Buddh Gaya,
dancing figures from Kausambi, Lakshmi from Pompeii and
the figures on the Mathura railing accentuate the beauty of
the human form without the inhibiting factors of clothes.
Around the waist is a heavy ornamentation, *kardhani*, while
the head sports a head gear, and a *tika* along the parting
of the hair and hanging on the forehead, heavy ear-rings,
rings, necklaces and bangles. The feet also sport a fair
amount of ringlets and anklets, the genesis of the *ghunghuroo*
(ankle bells). In the relief depicting the dance scene at Sanchi,
the men are seen sporting a wrap around the middle. The
dancer in the relief at Pawaya again sports a dhoti and a
head gear.

Interestingly, the figure of the dancing *nati* of Patliputra
(third century BC) seems to be wearing tight-fitting pyjamas
or pants and a flared frock. This costume is similar to the
churidar-angarkha worn by Kathak dancers today. In the
Mathura bas-relief, the *Sapta Matrikas* are seen wearing frocks
while in one of the coins of the Scythian ruler, Azilises,
even goddess Lakshmi ·is shown seated on a lotus wearing a
blouse and trousers.

A little later, once again, the Deogarh and Sanchi panels
of fifth century AD reveal the use of sewn clothes.
Interestingly, here again, the dancer is seen wearing tight-
pants upto the ankles (akin to the *churidar-pyjama* of today)
and a dress over it coming down below the knees. The ends
of a veil can also be discerned. This, once again, resembles
the dress popularly worn by some of the Kathak dancers of
today. Simultaneously, some of the regions saw the wearing
of *lehenga-choli* and the *dhoti-bandi* as can be seen in the
paintings of Bikaner of the fifth century AD. This, therefore,
bears out the fact that in ancient India, dancers were among
the few who wore stitched clothing.

By the 13th and 14th centuries, Muslim rule had been established in this belt and, therefore, the social conditions of the time were in a fluid state. The purdah system, wherein the women stayed behind the curtain or veil for protection, came to stay. Thus, no part of the woman's body was to be exposed. (Due to the extreme cold climate experienced in the north and north-west, the popular dresses were always long and covered most of the body.) Consequently, there was a slow change in the dress of the people. From the old tradition of unsewn clothes, the elongated piece of cloth was used to cover the torso and legs till the ankles with the other end covering the chest and head, like the *sari*. While *dhoti* loin cloth and *bandi* (shirt) came to be the dress of the men, the dress of the women over the pyjama as seen in the Deoghar reliefs as well as the *laughing nati* were two pieces: one for covering the chest and the second upto the ankles. A third piece, the *dupatta* covered the head and provided protection to the face from prying eyes. Thus, the *lehenga* (long skirt) and *choli* (blouse) came to stay.

However, the sculptures in the temples of Rajasthan during 12th-14th centuries again reveal the emphasis on the human form. How then does one explain the difference between the clothes of the common man and woman of this area to the portrayal of dancers and nymphs in the temples of Rajasthan? The latter were, perhaps, not symbolic or representative of the common dress of the period. It was, to some extent, a mirror of the revivalism of the 'tantric' philosophy and a concept with emphasis on the erotic beauty of the human form during the era of the *Bhakti Movement* (religious renaissance) in the country.

The later day paintings from Rajasthan and Kangra notably bring out certain modifications in the dressing habits. Elaborate hair-styles gave way to simplicity, highlighting the features of the beautiful maidens of the area. The *lehenga* (ankle-length-long flared skirt) became diaphanous accentuating the pleated strip of fan in front, and the sinuous grace of the body. The concept of 'beauty within the veil' as opposed to the earlier open concept of beauty was the keynote of medieval India.

Interestingly, the later medieval and early modern period paintings of Indian history pertaining to this region indicate that women dancers, predominantly in the Muslim courts, wore a full ankle length skirt (a divided long skirt or a *lehenga*) beneath a frock or an 'angarkha'.

The jewellery worn by the dancers or *natis* were the jewellery worn by the people, namely an elaborate *tika* (ornamentation adorning the parting of the hair), long as well as a short necklace, a '*kardhani*' (ornamentation around the waist), anklets, heavy bangles, rings and nose-rings or nose-pins. The ornaments could be made of gold, precious stones or studded with *kundan* (a transparent white precious stone) or of silver, reflecting the varied dressing habits of the people of the expansive Indo-Gangetic region.

The *Abhinaya Darpana* of Nandikesvara dwells on the fact that the physical attributes of a dancer are equally important. She should be slender-bodied, agile, young and self-confident. As stated in the following verse, the *ghunghuroos* (tiny bells) should be made of bronze having a pleasant tinkling sound; and at least a hundred or two hundred should be bound around each ankle with blue thread in tight knots:

suswarashca surupashca sookshma nakshatradevatah
kinkinyah kansyarachita ekaikangulikantaram
badhniyaannilasootren granthibhishca dridham punah
shatdwayam shatam vapi padyornatyakarini

In keeping with the theory and also to amplify the sound of the rhythmic intricacies of footwork and patterns executed by the dancer, a Kathak ties a minimum of hundred, which could go up to 200 or 250 ankle bells around each ankle. Leather belts on which ankle-bells are sewn are not used in Kathak as the use of leather is not sanctioned by tradition of the shastras and considered inauspicious in the context of Kathak which is a form of meditation and worship. This aspect was all the more important as the original Kathak priests performed in the temple precincts.

The instruments accompanying music and dance also underwent a change. The four different kinds of musical instruments are the *tata vadya* (stringed instruments such as the harp, veena, etc.), *sushira vadya* (wind instruments such as the flute, trumpet, etc.), *avanaddha vadya* (percussion instruments such as the pakhawaj, mridanga, damaru, etc.) and *ghana vadya* (solid instruments such as the cymbals). The material used to make the instruments provide clues to the flora and culture of the area: from the wood for the drum, hair for the bow, bamboo for the flute, etc. In India, the successive cultural groups and various currents of activity have resulted in the present cultural tradition. It is believed that the Aryans brought with them the flute (*venu*) and the harp (*veena*) which they used in vedic rituals and it is held that the Savaras were inventors of the flute.

In the sculpturesque reliefs of ancient India, at least, three varieties of musical instruments have been shown accompanying the dancers. While the stringed instruments and the drums are featured in all the reliefs, at least one of the remaining two varieties, the wind instruments and the solid instruments has been depicted. Only in a few reliefs can the presence of all four varieties be ascertained. The Bharhut, Mathura and Deogarh panels reveal the presence of cymbals, seven stringed harp and the drum held horizontally.

The Sanchi and the Pawaya reliefs reveal the presence of two drummers, one holding the drum horizontally and the second holding the drum vertically as well as the presence of musicians playing wind instruments (such as the double pipe or the flute or carved trumpets) and the stringed instruments such as the harp. The Pawaya and Ajanta reliefs reveal the use of a pair of vertical drums.

According to mythology, Lord Ganesh is said to have made the pakhawaj out of the earth and the skin from the demon Baktasur. In another story, in the paradise of Indra, the gandharva who played the pakhawaj, due to his arrogance,

Dancers and musicians in a panel from Pawaya near Gwalior.

earned the curse of Indra and took birth on the earth near Benaras, where he taught the art of playing the *mridanga* (also called the *pakhawaj*) to the children of a paan-seller who popularised the art of *pakhawaj* playing. In another version, Swati Rishi is said to have created the *pakhawaj*. This instrument, however, has been known by various names.

Mridanga, derived from the word *mrid* (earth) and *anga* (element of the earth), is a general classification denoting drums of the *ankya* family made out of the earth.

Interestingly, even now in eastern Uttar Pradesh and Bihar, the *ankya* drum is still known as the *mridanga* while the name *pakhawaj* is more prevalent in western Uttar Pradesh, Delhi and the neighbouring areas.

In the *Natyashastra*, Bharata has referred to the indispensability of the drum. Even though the 'damru' (an hourglass shaped drum identified with Lord Shiva) is considered the primordial drum, yet Bharata gives an interesting legend regarding the origin of drums: once when Sage Swati went to the lake to fetch water, Lord Indra sent a downpour of torrential rain. In the lake, the falling rain made various sounds on the leaves of the lotus and the waters which inspired the sage to create drums from wood and earth with help from the heavenly architect, Vishvakarma. Bharata further elucidates the inter-relationship of music and rhythm in the following manner: 'Noise coming out first from the human body goes to the wooden veena and then they go to the puskara and the solid instruments. Strokes on them by various movements are to be known as giving shelter to words.'

The medieval period in India witnessed great developments in the cultural traditions of the country. Due to political and social changes, the impact on the development of musical instruments could not be ruled out. While the invention of many new instruments such as the tabla or the sitar, in the form in which we know them today, developed during this period and were attributed to Amir Khusro, yet there is no evidence to this effect. His own writings or those of his contemporaries do not mention this fact. However, his dominant personality and interest in art has probably given rise to the theory.

The *tabla* is basically a two piece drum played vertically. While the right piece is called the *tabla*, the left piece is known as the *bayan* or *dagga*. Both the tabla and the pakhawaj are made of wood with a stretched skin parchment at the mouth in the centre of which is a loading of black paste. This practice of applying the paste, known even in earlier times as the technique of applying *vilepana*, has been discussed in the *Natyashastra*. Many scholars, thus, believe that the tabla was an adaptation of the pair of vertical drums seen in the ancient sculptural reliefs of 5th-7th centuries AD though the name could have been influenced by *tabl*, a kind of Persian drum. The Persian *tabl* is a very large drum struck with small padded sticks on both sides. Similarly, the *thaval* of southern India is also a large drum tapering on both sides where the right side is played by hand and the left with a drum stick. However, within Persia itself, the most popular drum which is still being widely used today since the last many centuries, is the *tonbak*, a one piece, vertical drum resting on a slender pillar. This has recently been modified to add a steel ring tuning device in order to be able to adjust to the basic nodal tonic of a *dastgah* music.

Tabla itself is an anagram of 'ta' for 'taal' (rhythm), 'ba' for 'baant' (rhythmic patterns) and 'la' for 'laya' (tempo).

Another popular story regarding the invention of tabla is attributed to the rivalry between Sudhar Khan Dhodi and Bhagwandas, both reputed pakhawaj players of their times. In a fit of anger, Dhodi is reputed to have dashed his pakhawaj to the ground which broke into two pieces resulting in the two-piece drum called the tabla. The sound of the tabla is lighter and sweeter than the grave and serious note emanating from the pakhawaj.

The tabla seems to have become the main percussion instrument, rather late, for Abul Fazal who, in his *Ain-e-Akbari*, mentions the pakhawaj in the orchestra accompanying the dancers. Similarly, the Mughal miniature paintings or the paintings of Gujarat, Rajasthan and Kangra the schools also indicate the 'pakhawaj' as the main percussion instrument of the dancers.

The fretted lutes which can be commonly seen in the ancient sculptures could have been the precursor of the sitar. The figure of the veena player from Ahichchhatra (fifth century AD) shows the existence of a harp very similar to the mandolin used today or the *oud*, the deep bellied lute from Persia. However, the word *sitar* is usually taken to be derived from the Persian word *seh-tar* (three strings). On the other hand, the *sarod* is an adaptation of the *rabab*.

In Malaysia, the rebab is a descendent of the lyra of the Byzantines. This is a bow instrument with three strings resembling somewhat the Rajasthani *kamaicha* unlike the Indian sarod which is a plucked instrument. The Malaysian rebab functions predominantly as a rhythmic and drone accompaniment and partly as melodic in some local dance theatres.

Thus, the traditional instruments accompanying dance in the Indus Gangetic region included two kinds of drums: the pakhawaj and the pair of vertical drums, a stringed instrument such as the lute and a flute or a cymbal player. After the 'invention' of many new instruments during the medieval period, the accompanying instruments to a Kathak performance is taken from the wide array of instruments available. They include the *tabla* and *pakhawaj* among the percussion instruments while the vocalist normally uses the *tanpura* (a stringed instrument giving the basic notes) or a *harmonium* (a form of a harmonica based on the principle of a wind instrument). Amongst the other instruments normally used are the *sarangi* (a bow stringed instrument), *sitar* and *sarod* (both being plucked stringed instruments), the flute and the cymbals.

A usual performance would consist of four to five musicians which would include one or two percussionists on the tabla and pakhawaj, a vocalist and two instrumentalists. The costume worn by the dancer could be the *lehenga-choli* the *churidar-angarkha* or the *sari* depending on the performer's choice. The ornamentation would include the tika on the forehead, ear-rings, necklaces, bangles, rings and a waist-band. About two hundred ankle-bells on strings adorn each ankle. The make-up is slightly heavy accentuating the brows and the eyes in order to highlight the emotions being portrayed by a mere glance or a flick of an eyebrow. The tips of the hand and feet are painted red with *alta* (a red washable fluid) or *henna* which again serves the purpose of highlighting the *mudras* (gestures) and poses.

Patronage and Schools

The centres of art witnessed a shift in the successive ages even though the art form was spread over the entire Indus-Gangetic belt. This was brought about by the mobility of the people and the artistes, due to shifting patronage and the dynamics of inherent development. The centres especially for dance had covered Vaishali, Magadh, Patliputra, Mathura, Rajasthan, Bundelkhand, Allahabad and Varanasi. However, in the post Aurangzeb period, there was a great loosening up of attitudes towards music and dance and consequently, pockets of patronage sprang up in various parts of the Indo-Gangetic belt as the local rajas, maharajas and nawabs evinced interest in the promotion of art and culture. In the last two centuries, the predominant pockets of influence were Lucknow and Jaipur which also led to the establishment of the 'gharana' system. 'Gharana' has been derived from the word *ghar* meaning house. It was the patronage extended by great art patrons and music lovers such as Nawab Wajid Ali Shah of Lucknow (Avadh) and the Rajas of Jodhpur and Jaipur which led to a concentration of artistes in these areas. In the 20th century, new pockets of patronage included, besides Lucknow and Jaipur, Raigarh, Benaras, Allahabad and in more recent times, Delhi. Each family or house concentrated on their environment. While the Lucknow gharana made grace (*lasya*) their forte, *tandava* or the virile became the hallmark of the Jaipur gharana. For a 'gharana' to emerge, what were required were consistently good dancers with the profession being handed down from generation to generation carrying with each gharana an element of emphasis in addition to sustained patronage.

The identification of the gharana with a place rather than with individuals came about at the end of the 19th century (around 1895) when most active patronage centred around Lucknow, Jaipur and Benaras. Even though other places like Raigarh, Jodhpur, Bettiah and Patna did provide the necessary impetus for artistes to flourish, yet as the artistes patronised by the rulers of these places were offshoots either as part of the family tree or as disciples of the old established gharanas, no name of any new gharana cropped up. Today, as most of the artistes (of all Indian classical dance styles) are concentrated in and around Delhi, they are constantly subjected to external influences which have left this imprint in the presentation and repertoire of this dance forms. Thus, there is a slow emergence of a new terminology: the Delhi gharana in Kathak which still requires a considerable span of time before becoming an accepted school of Kathak.

In 1722, Sadat Khan was appointed the Subedar of Avadh by the Mughal Emperor Muhammed Shah. It was during the rule of Asaf-ud-daulah (1775 to 1798) that the formal introduction of Kathak in the courts began to catch attention, even though it appears that one Khushi Maharaj performed during the time of Shuja-ud-daulah. Sometimes in the early part of the 19th century, Prakashji Misra, grandson of Ishwari Prasadji, a Kathak of the temple of Hadia tehsil near Allahabad, migrated to the court of Asaf-ud-daulah in Lucknow. It is stated that having lost his parents within a short span of time in tragic circumstances, he was disillusioned and, therefore, moved away from his native place near Allahabad. This move laid the foundations for the Lucknow gharana as his son Durga Prasad became not only the court dancer but also the guru of Nawab Wajid Ali Shah during the latter's short reign (1847-1856). Culturally, his brief period of rule saw the golden period of art and culture as dancers, poets and musicians regained their lost grandeur. Wajid Ali Shah is remembered fondly in the annals of art history not only as a great patron but also as a sensitive poet and a proficient Kathak disciple who danced the various pieces especially the *thaat ang* with precision, sensitivity and grace. Furthermore, he is credited with having staged many 'Rahas' based on the 'Ras-leelas'.

With this new impetus given to Kathak practitioners, the environment in which they performed cast a subtle influence on the presentation of the dance. The Muslim court etiquette with its emphasis on grace (*nazakat*), delicacy, simplicity and elegance of movements as intrinsic features in presentation alongwith the superficial external features of the costume prevalent in Muslim culture were adapted by the Kathaks in the Avadh court. This became the hallmark of the Lucknow school that was handed down from generation to generation, so much so that elegance of *ang* imbued with '*rasanubhiti*' have influenced the *katha* presentation of the later part of the 20th century. On the other hand, the sombreness and the ethos associated with the culture and rituals prevalent in the courts of the Hindu maharajahs and rajas of Rajasthan and eastern Uttar Pradesh dwelt upon the practical presentation of dance, shorn of the frills of excessive Muslim court etiquette, lending it an air which was not reminiscent

of the heavily scented, luxurious and leisurely pace associated
with Avadh.

As Nawab Wajid Ali Shah was a gifted poet, musician
and dancer, he laid great emphasis on the execution of *thaats*
and the delicacy associated with every flick of the wrist,
heaving of the chest to the basic rhythmic mnemonics and
the poise of stance. He wrote *thumris* under the pen name
of 'Akhtar' and 'Piya'. Some of the memorable verses written
by him include:

> *Mohan rasiya aye bagiya, choom rahi ras kali kali re,*
> *koyi kali Hari nam pukare, koyi kali sun Ali Ali re..*

(Mohan, the beloved, has come into the garden and has
kissed the lips of the flowers; while some call out to
Him, others are intoxicated by His voice...)

> *babul mora naihara chhooto ri jaye...*

(O friend, I leave my parents' home behind me...)

The 'nritta' sequences, the pure rhythmic patterns in the
Lucknow school boasted of clarity, precision and finesse in
execution. Efforts were also made to simplify the most
difficult of rhythmic patterns which laid the foundations for
the *ginati ki tihais* (*tihais* executed to numerals). Even the
gats or gaits were given particular attention by the Nawab
with due care being taken in its execution by a *zanana*
(feminine) or a *mardana* (masculine). Details of such gaits
have been enunciated in various works such as 'Banni' and
'Najo' by the Nawab. From the *Kanun-e-Mausiki*, it appears
that there was an over-emphasis on the expressional execution
of *gats* which, at times, were interchangeable with the *thaats*.
The poet within Wajid Ali Shah naturally gave impetus to
the singing of *thumris* and *ghazals* whereby a myriad

interpretations of a word or line of text became the hallmark of expressional sequences leading to the full flowering of the *bhav batana* by the dancers of Lucknow. As a natural corollary, most of the dancers of the Lucknow gharana were also adept at singing with strong leanings towards Vaishnavism, especially in the enactment of Krishna episodes.

Like Uttar Pradesh, Rajasthan too had been a great centre for music and dance. In the *Mahabharata*, Uttara, daughter of the King of the Matsya region (near present day Alwar), was initiated into the art of dance by Arjun, disguised as Brihanalla. Closer to our times, Amber, which had been established by a Kachhwaha prince sometime in the 11th century AD, saw patronage to music, dance and paintings by Raja Mansingh I in the 16th century. While *Ragamanjari*, a text on music and dance, was composed by Pundrik Vitthal under the patronage of Madho Singh, *Hastak-Ratnavali*, a text on dance was composed in the 17th century (1673 AD) during the reign of Maharaja Ram Singh. In the *guni-jan-khana* (abode of experts or treasure of virtuosos) established as a system by Maharaja Jai Singh in the 18th century AD, it is believed that over seven hundred and fifty artistes were given patronage. Its records reveal the presence of 10 male Kathaks and 38 women dancer-singers during the reign of Maharaja Sawai Madho Singh II. Another important text on music and dance, the *Radha Govinda Sangitasar* was written by a group of four scholars under the patronage of Maharaja Sawai Pratap Singh towards the end of the 18th century; he himself was a gifted musician and poet writing under the pen name of 'Brijnidhi'. Thus, besides the dancers attached to the various temples like the temple of Govind Deoji, there were the court dancers maintained in the *guni-jan-khana* and in the *zenana* who performed on various social and religious occasions.

The ethos of the gharana as it developed in this area was very different from the trappings of the Muslim court of

Avadh as is evident from the fact that Bhanuji, one of the early figures in the Jaipur gharana lineage, being a devotee of Shiva, was well-known for his rendition of the *Shiva tandava*. With Vaishnav influence on other branches of the family, Krishna themes became equally important. The *Khiskan* and the *kasak-masak* in *thaat* alongwith complexities of rhythmic patterns became the hallmark of this gharana from Rajasthan, which slowly came to be known as the Jaipur gharana after a meeting of the Kathaks in 1895 when it was decided that henceforth the gharanas would be named after a place instead of families or individuals.

While there was mimetic enactment to the recitation of a 'kavitt' in the Jaipur gharana, symbolic of the 'vachikabhinaya' of the *Natyashastra*, the Lucknow gharana brought to the fore the lyricism, sensitivity and grace in the enactment of the *kavitt* which was sung, usually without accompaniment of rhythm, *khula gayan*. The *tatkar* in the Jaipur gharana is rendered with the full striking of the feet whereas in the Lucknow gharana, it is executed with a beautiful heel-feet combination.

The easy mobility of the Kathaks from Rajasthan led to their migration to a number of places either as teachers or as court dancers or as students. While some of them such as Pt. Sunder Prasadji, son of Chunnilal, became the disciple of Bindadin Maharaj at Lucknow, Janaki Prasad, a Kathak from Bikaner, migrated to Benaras and laid the foundations of the Janaki Prasad gharana later known as the Benaras gharana. Dularamji, son of Hukamji, migrated to the court of Bettiah in Bihar while his sons, Biharilalji and Hiralalji, spent a number of years at Indore with their brother Puranlal going over to Bombay.

The predominant feature of the Janaki Prasad gharana is the emphasis on the *natwari bols* of rhythmic patterns based only on mnemonics of dance without dilution from the inclusion of tabla or pakhawaj syllables. In the *tatkar*, emphasis is placed on the heel movement. The *thirkan* alongwith the *chamak* (lightning) and *kat tarash* (fine executions) are some of the keynotes associated with this gharana. Another notable feature is that of the *angikabhinaya* where feelings have to emanate from every pore of the body even with the back to the audience. This particular aspect is also given great emphasis in the Lucknow style where minimal movements seek to convey the maximum emotion.

As in the Jaipur gharana, virtuosity was shown in the Benaras gharana with the *thararara* movement of the toe, resembling the ringing of tiny bells. Similarly, the *chakra bhramari*, usually performed from the left has been performed from the right by dancers of this gharana with equal dexterity.

Traditionally, unlike Rajasthan and Uttar Pradesh, Raigarh had no popular tradition of classical music and dance; however, there was a rich folk culture available in the region due to its close proximity to the states of Bihar, Orissa and Andhra Pradesh. Even though there were stray influences from the cultures of the Ikshvaku dynasty of Ayodhya to the Satavahanas, the Guptas of the fourth century AD till the Ratanpur dynasty of the Kalachuris, it was only with Raja Bhupdeo Singh that classical music and dance, especially Kathak and North Indian classical music, came to the fore. Pandit Chunnilal and Shivnarain were in the court of Raja Bhupdeo Singh while Jailal, a Kathak from Jaipur, spent eight years in the court of Raja Chakradhar Singh of Raigarh in the early part of the 20th century. Here, among the eminent dancers who had received training from the dancer-gurus from Rajasthan were Kartikram, Anujram and Kalyan.

Under the patronage of Raja Bhupdeo Singh and his sons, Raja Chakradhar Singh (also known as Nanhe Maharaj) and Natwar Singh, many books on poetry and prose such as *Kavyakanan, Ramyarasa, Nagma-e-Farhat, Josh-e-Farhat* were written. On the subject of music and dance, Raja Chakradhar Singh himself compiled a dance treatise called *Nartan*

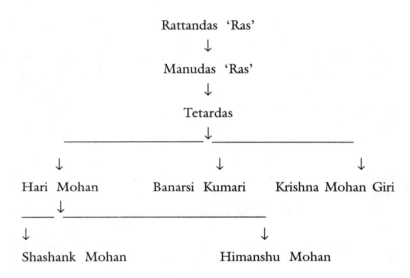

Rattandas 'Ras'
↓
Manudas 'Ras'
↓
Tetardas
↓

↓   ↓   ↓
Hari Mohan   Banarsi Kumari   Krishna Mohan Giri
↓

↓   ↓
Shashank Mohan   Himanshu Mohan

Sarwaswam, the manuscript of which weighed six and a half kilograms! A tala treatise *Talatyonidhi* (weighing thirty six kilograms) and treatises on the tabla and the pakhawaj called *tabla-pushpakara* (weighing three and a half kilograms) and *murajaparan-pushpakara.*

At Mithila, Raja Sheo Singh (1417-1576) encouraged the enactment of *padas* (verses) of Vidyapati and Jayat while the interest of Maharaja Shubhankar (1516-1607) manifested itself not only in the performances of artistes of his time but also in his authorship of *Sri Hastamuktavali*, a treatise on hand gestures utilised in dance. (Due to a curse on the Mithila rulers, the succession to the throne has never been direct, at least in the last ten generations or so, and the throne was inherited by the adopted son.) The rulers at Bettiah came into prominence as great patrons of dance and music with Raja Gaj Singh (1659-1694), yet the two most well-known names were those of Maharaja Anand Kishore Singh (1816-1875) and Maharaja Nawal Kishore Singh (1835-1855), as they were not only great patrons but great artistes themselves.

Many compositions written by them were enacted by the artistes of their times. In 1814, Buchanan's survey mentions over 58 Kathak establishments in the towns of Bihar.

The zamindars of Jamira estate at Arrah emerged as great patrons of the 19th and 20th century as four generations saw their 'haveli' (small palace) resounding to the sound of ankle bells and music. But the most outstanding of them was Shatrunjaya Prasad Singh alias Lallanji. Lallanji was honoured with many awards and titles including the 'Mridanga Chakra Choodamani' and the 'Laya Bhaskar'.

Similarly, even though many Kathaks moved to various places or durbars in Bihar (Baneli, Gaya, Darbhanga, Naugachhia, Gidhaur, Muzaffarpur, Patna) and other parts of Madhya Pradesh like Indore or received training from Bindadin Maharaj or Achhan Maharaj of Lucknow, yet no distinct school of Kathak emerged in these areas, unlike the field of music where distinct schools such as the Gaya school of music and the Darbhanga school of dhrupad and pakhawaj had emerged. Perhaps, to a certain extent, besides branches of the Jaipur gharana, Benaras gharana and Lucknow gharana, mention could be made of the Rattan Das Ras family of Samastipur whose origins lay in the continuation of the Ras-leela tradition with heavy emphasis on traditional Kathak representation.

The social and political atmosphere in Bihar led to an emphasis on the panchpatiya system and as vocalists and instrumentalists received wider patronage than dance, the rendering of dance patterns also emphasised the rhythmic aspect. The rhythmic patterns of Kathak taught by Lallanji at Arrah or Lakshmi Narayanji, Gopalji and Pannalalji at Naugachhia, Mohanlalji at Gidhaur and Shivlal and Heeralalji at Darbhanga indicate a wide variety of *bols* based on the tonal and aural sounds of nature very akin to the pieces danced at Raigarh. Here too, patterns revolved around the *bijli-paran, ashva-paran, dawanal-paran, jhoola-paran* and the *mahawat-paran* bringing to the fore a fine display of rhythmic permutations involving various *jatis.*

With the passage of time, despite concentration of certain usages of rhythmic patterns becoming distinct in the different gharanas, it is a noteworthy fact that even within a gharana, stylisation of the *ang* (body movements) have taken place to such an extent in succeeding generations imparting a flavour variant to the earlier one but maintaining the style of the particular gharana.

Today, with the concentration of a number of major dancers and gurus in Delhi, a distinct style has evolved within the Kathak fold emphasising neatness of lines, *angas,* alongwith grace and technical brilliance, blurring the erstwhile clear distinctions between the various gharanas to some extent. This has become a trend setter in many ways to practitioners of Kathak in different parts of the country.

Within each gharana, the lineology is extensive. The Lucknow gharana which was established with the moving of Prakashji Mishra from Hadia tehsil near Allahabad to Lakshmanpur (the old name for Lucknow), saw a great dancer in Ishwari Prasad, grandfather of Prakashji Mishra. Notable successors of Prakashji Mishra included his sons Durga Prasad and Thakur Prasad and his grandsons, Bindadin Maharaj, Kalka Prasad and Bhairon Prasad. Bindadin was bestowed with the title of Maharaj (King of kings among the dancers) which was decided in the meeting of the Kathaks in 1895 to be given to a person with over 100 disciples who was at the same time an adept at dancing, singing, teaching, playing instruments and composing songs. He is reputed to have written over 1500 thumris. The sons of Kalka Prasad Achhan Maharaj, Lachhu Maharaj and Shambhu Maharaj were stars in the Kathak firmament. While Achhan Maharaj's forte was *nritta,* Lachhu Maharaj's forte was grace and Shambhu Maharaj earned for himself the title of King of Abhinaya. Birju Maharaj, the son of the late Shri

Achhan Maharaj, is a versatile genius being not only a dancer with an inimitable style of his own but also a gifted vocalist and a percussionist on whom numerous awards and honours have been conferred for his unparalleled contributions to Kathak.

The Jaipur gharana, in turn, has many branches of lineages. However, it is commonly believed that Bhanuji who was a devotee of Lord Shiva, was the father of this gharana. His grandson Kanuji was influenced by the Krishna bhakti (devotion to Lord Krishna) in Vrindavan and incorporated it within his dance. Kanuji's grandsons, Hari Prasad and Hanuman Prasad were well-known as the *Devpari ka jora* (pair of celestial artistes) and became dancers in the *Gunijan -khana* (abode of the experts) of the Jaipur court. The sons of Hanuman Prasad—Mohan Lal, Chiranjilal and Narayan Prasad—were considered great dancers of their time. In a parallel development, their cousins, Jailal and Sunder Prasad, sons of Chunni Lal, also left an indelible stamp of their greatness as dancers, the former having died young but the latter living long enough to win many coveted awards.

As far as the Benaras gharana is concerned, there are two distinct lineages. The first one is the Jankiprasad gharana which owes its name to the fact that the originator, Pt. Jankiprasad, though hailing from the Churu-Sujangarh area of Rajasthan, made Benaras his home. Some of the illustrious names of this gharana were Ganeshi Lal, Hiralal, Hanuman Prasad, Sukhdev and Kundan Lal.

The second Benaras gharana refers to Pt. Sukhdev Maharaj, who, like Pt. Jankiprasad, made Benaras his home. He, his daughters Tara, Alaknanda and Sitara Devi and his grandson Gopi Krishna, have made valuable contributions to Kathak. Septuagenarian Sitara Devi is an example of vivacity, stamina and tenacity of purpose in her pursuit and propagation of Kathak.

Some of the other notable dancers in Kathak were Damayanti Joshi known for her remarkable grace, Roshan Kumari for her technical brilliance and Krishan Kumar for his electrifying presence. Kumudini Lakhia has made valuable contributions by introducing innovative choreography in the dance form. Besides these artistes, the Kathak firmament is full of bright stars and illustrious veterans, and it would be impossible to list their names as each is a talent to contend with.

Changing Aesthetics

Kathak dance which was born in the temples of the Indus Gangetic belt over three thousand years ago has passed through many vicissitudes. In the development of the dance form, a continuity is discerned in the basic stance and poses adopted as evident from the few remaining sculptures of ancient India as most of the temples had been ravaged by invaders. The range of movements, the use of expressions and hand-gestures have always been highly developed as the Kathak, a solo dance-preacher, needed all such ingredients in order to be able to communicate the mythological stories and their inner meanings to the gathered congregation.

Parallel to its growth, the course of classical Hindustani music and the literature of this region had a deep impact on the dance form as no dance cannot remain void of musical and textual content. The social dressing habits had their influence on the costumes adopted by the dancers. The instruments too underwent changes in the succeeding ages.

The shifting centres of art and the patronage extended to the artistes led to the establishment of the gharana system and increased the technical brilliance and sophistication in execution and presentation of the dance.

Kathak is a dance form which lends itself very easily to innovations. Many ballets, dance-dramas and group compositions on traditional themes have been enacted, in addition to which contemporary and abstract themes have been attempted with great success. Pace, creativity and innovation have been great and have taken the dance form to newer and greater heights. The story-telling tradition, the natural stance of Kathak and the emphasis on various local languages besides Sanskrit have contributed to many new experiments and an expansion of the repertoire. As a result of the possibility of using any language, Sanskrit gave way to the local dialects used by the poets of the Bhakti Movement which again facilitated the inclusion of Urdu poetry like ghazal besides contemporary verses in Khari Hindi or Hindustani.

Every age has defined beauty differently. While the pencil thin eyebrows of the 40s of this century made a brief comeback for about a decade in the 70s, the detailed execution of every curvature in sculpture gave way to simplicity and directness of expression. The trend in the 60s saw a lessening of the arm movements while executing patterns at a fast tempo. The 80s and the 90s saw a further reduction in the extension of the arms while dancing at fast tempos. Similarly, the position of the elbows which assumed a higher position in the basic yogic position has been lowered over the years. Movement of the present generation of dancers of the 80s and 90s vary greatly from the dancers of earlier generations even within the same gharana.

In terms of presentation too, the emphasis on footwork, pirouettes and lengthy displays of rhythmic passages prevalent during the middle part of the century has now been replaced by a balanced emphasis on its natural story-telling tradition.

Items such as dancing on the edge of a brass plate or on a bed of nails (Jaipur and Benaras gharanas) have now been weeded out of the present day Kathak repertoire.

The status of dancers has been greatly influenced by the social conditions of different ages. The ancient period saw a predominance of women dancers in the Gangetic belt such as Amrapali, Roopkosha, Salvati, Vimla, Padmavati, Upkosha and Satunuka. These courtesan-dancers supposedly enjoyed a high position in society. The medieval period saw the flag of Kathak flying with many male dancers coming to the fore; but owing to the wide exploitation of the women dancers and the purdah system, the status of dancers declined. With the new cultural and social consciousness, the arts have regained their lost glory and many women and male dancers dot the Kathak scenario today.

Innovation in any dance form goes hand-in-hand with a purpose, for it has to have an aim and direction. The innate ability and capacity of Kathak to imbibe the ethos of the changing times is one of its greatest assets, for it is this quality more than any other that has helped in the enrichment of the dance. Another phenomenon observed is that certain movements or parts of the repertoire which may have been a common practice in a certain age may have lost its relevance in the succeeding ages and which may have again been reincorporated in a subsequent age. Perhaps, some of the elements of reincorporation could broadly fall under the modern term 'innovation'. However, with constant usage it comes to be accepted as tradition.

In the case of the *tarana* which emerged due to the influence of Sufism, a state of ecstasy in the union of the soul with God, words become meaningless and thus the phrases of 'ta-na-na-na' or 'deem-de-re-na' are repetitive and hypnotic and its inclusion in the Kathak repertoire in the last few centuries has now become part of tradition. Just before and after the beginning of the Christian calendar, it appears that dancing on the tip of needles and on the edge of a brass plate were innovations which seem to have been lost in the subsequent centuries, to re-emerge in western India in the last few centuries, only to be discontinued by the Kathak of the second half of the 20th century.

I remember hearing of the great doyen Pt. Sunder Prasadji's performance on 'gulal' in his award winning function over 30 years ago, when he drew the pattern of Ganesh while dancing a Ganesh paran. If such an item is performed within any dance form today, it may, perhaps, be perceived as innovative.

Increasingly, Kathaks have been choosing to delineate emotions and *abhinaya* through items and themes which range from the abstract to a depiction of the contemporary ethos; modern interpretations of ancient mythologies; and the exposition of 'thumris', which have persisted for the last 200 years or so replacing the age-old 'dhrupad-dhamar'. To illustrate this further, on the abstract front, either a mood or an occasion or situation could form the basic subject around which an expressional or a rhythmic item could evolve. For example, 'galaxy' or 'spring' could be represented rhythmically or through suggestive situations bringing out the essence of each of the items.

Social issues such as environment, integration or situations relating to caste or untouchability and human rights have been taken up by Kathak artistes. Similarly, modern interpretations of mythological episodes such as that of the disrobing of Draupadi (likened to the deforesting of the earth) and the subjugation of Kaliya, the serpent living in the river Yamuna, by Lord Krishna in the 'Kaliyadaman' (likened to the cleaning up of a polluted river) have been rendered in Kathak. Besides, contemporary poetry has also found its way into the Kathak repertoire.

Traditionally, kathak by its very nature of story-telling is a solo dance form with only its offshoot, the 'ras-leela' being a group composition. However, in the last 60-70 years particularly, a parallel stream of composition, not only as 'solo' pieces but also as 'group compositions', has been noticeable. Here, traditional as well as modern, abstract and contemporary themes could be delineated through the medium of group or solo compositions. This, therefore, takes it beyond the usual 'jugalbandis' (duets) or a simple dance ballet or a dance-drama. With the advent of narrative-heavy texts, enactment of such a piece through the medium of dance and recitation would appropriately fall under the category of 'dance-enactment'.

Various dance enactments based on incidents in the lives of Mahatma Gandhi, sage Ramana Maharshi, sage Ramkrishna Paramhansa and Swami Vivekanand have been performed.

Incidentally, the dance-drama within the Kathak framework was not unknown. The 'Ras-leela' of Vrindaban which originated during the Bhakti Movement and later the 'Rahas' of Nawab Wajid Ali Shah in the 19th century were based on Kathak.

Further, the possibility of expression through every limb of the body has been explored. For example, through a variety of footwork (*tatkar*) or feet placements or sometimes through the medium of hand gestures alone (with the rest of the body kept in the dark) an item has been delineated, bringing out the innate meaning and beauty of the concept. The basic philosophy behind such a representation is that '*rasa*' or emotion is visible in every minor limb of the body and is not confined to the body as a whole.

Usage of slides of photographs or paintings on the screen or the paintings itself as well as the correlation with theatre have been experimented with by many Kathak dancers.

The space available to the dancer has varied from age to age giving it a certain framework which lent a necessary definition to the movements practised within the dance form. Performing within the confines of a temple and performing in the more spacious court of the Nawab or Raja necessarily gave two different limitations of space to the dancer and intelligently the movements were patterned to meet the space requirement accordingly. Modern technology has bestowed a large stage in an auditorium on the dancer with vast resources of space, both horizontally and vertically. Thus, perforce, the dancer has to take advantage of the vastness of space available all around and the feet movements alongwith arm patterns have adapted to the new setting of the modern auditoria.

In this aspect, the phenomenon of disappearance and reappearance of some movements is visible. Some of the movements such as the *urdhvajanu* (or the lifting of the leg) which, though practised by ordinary Kathaks but not encouraged within a court, were lost sight of due to the overshadowing of the common man's Kathak by the highly patronised court version. The Braj (Gangetic belt) literature of the medieval period and the *kirtaniyas* and *kathakiyas* of this period depict Krishna in poses like *lallita, tribhangi, natwara, girdhari*, along with gaits such as the *udghata, sanel* and *mrigamaral*. Even the dance scene paintings in the Padishahanama reveal poses which include the *ardhamandali, tribhangi*, etc. Today, these are reappearing in some display such as in the galloping movement of horses or in an extensive display of an angry Shiva.

Similarly, the combination of a slight dip and skip movement performed in an extremely gracious manner and the heave-shove movement denoting toil and labour as well as the extended arm movements with sinuous up and down movements combined with alternate dipping of the knees in order to denote the flight of birds have also come into vogue. Expressions through the tension and release of the body highlighted by extensive extension of the legs wherever required have come to be recognised by the thinking artistes of today who have realised that the body is not only a vehicle of movement but also as a storehouse of expression. Even the throwing of the hands in the air to highlight agony, pain or despair has been utilised, thus extending the vocabulary of body movements and meeting the demands of the modern provocation of space utilisation and the desire to emote the innermost emotions freely and effectively.

Necessity to depict a certain object, a person or a situation has prompted the emergence of new hand gestures and thus additions were reflected in the Abhinaya Darpan over the older *Natyashastra*. The horizon has expanded further in *SriHastamuktavali* with many more additions in the various hand gestures including the *nritta hastas*. Even though guns or drugs have been known for some time yet its usage or depiction in a usual dance repertoire was not so common though the sword or an indirect reference to drugs has been depicted. However, with today's increasing violence and drug addiction, such themes depicting this concern have also found their way into dance compositions. In such a situation, the prevailing gamut of single or combined hand gestures do not adequately meet the demand, leading, therefore, to the innovation of newer combined hand gestures.

Even though steeped in the Hindustani classical music system and coursing a parallel chart, the instruments utilised in Kathak have been keeping pace with the changing times. From the age-old *pakhawaj* and the *veena, tabla, harmonium, sarod* and the *sitar* are some of the familiar accompaniments today in a rendering of traditional Kathak. But in some of the new compositions, electronic music has been utilised. This type of music, the compositions of which are within the Hindustani classical framework but executed through electronic instruments, have been particularly favoured in the recording of music for dance-ballets and dance-enactments. The arguments or situational necessity in its favour are many. A particular dance ballet requiring a complex music composition would automatically presuppose a host of musical effects and musicians. Secondly, keeping today's preoccupation of the artistes, the dancer or the choreographer finds it nearly impossible to hold a number of rehearsals with 15-20 musicians together. In such a situation, recording of the musical score not only eases the problem but also enables proper rehearsals for the large cast of dancers, leading to a more perfect rendering on stage.

On another plane, many compositions within the Kathak style have been attempted—and successfully—on musical scores other than the Hindustani classical style. Therefore, it is not surprising to find Kathak compositions being danced to Thyagaraja's kritis in the Carnatic style or to western classical pieces by Schubert, Ravel or Debussy. In each of these compositions, the responsive mood evoked by the music in turn provoked the creative faculties of the dancer, thereby proving the universality of the language of music and dance as they create an atmosphere suitable to the emotions engulfing one and all. While rendering such pieces, appropriate musical instruments related to the musical piece are used so as to minimise any danger of aesthetic dilution on this account. In case some of these compositions required maintenance of a mood of silence and serenity, the dancer had to be bold enough to cast off the *ghunghuroos* for such an item so as to respect the mood of the musical score and the instrument. To an initially stunned audience used to the sound of ankle-bells, the melancholic beauty of the sound of silence would slowly engulf them in its warm web where the faculties focus and enjoy the fluidity of the movements and the composition of the dance.

During the staging of an evening "Moonlight Impressionism" in 1993 based on an Indian folk tale of a night flower, rendered to a string of Western classical music compositions of Ravel and Debussy on the piano by Herman Sausen and interspersed with brilliant music compositions by Pt. Jwala Prasad, the decision to cast off the ankle-bells was prompted by the need to be able to hear the soft piano strains as the pianist was adamant on not using a microphone.

Similarly, in the rendering of the ballet 'Muktilekha' on human rights in 1987, *ghunghuroos* had to be dispensed with; but the dance renderings to pieces of Schubert and Otto Farber and the Russian song 'Cacusha' in 1980 utilised the ankle-bells.

Even in the usage of language as a tool of communication falling within the classification of *vacikabhinaya*, Kathaks, in their renderings, have reflected the popular language or dialect of the society of the time as was evident while discussing the development of language as symbolised in Kathak poetics. In keeping with this tradition, the Kathaks of today have chosen to represent and enact their emotions transcending language barriers and, thus, usage of popular Hindi, English, Tamil and Telugu are not unknown in Kathak renderings. The frontiers of language have also been extended to interpretations of poetry written in foreign (non-Indian) languages.

The *aharyabhinaya* has played a key role in the aesthetics of dance and the Kathaks have tried to balance the requirements of the call of beauty and aesthetics within the dance with the social attire of the day. Today, the emphasis of the dancer ranges from the traditional *lehenga-choli* or *churidar-angarkha* with heavy costume jewellery and make-up to the simplest of costumes with no excessive ornamentation. This is particularly visible in dance-dramas and thematic enactments where from a very exaggerated heavy costume and ornamentation patronised by dancers of yesteryear, it has given way to simplicity in the costume and ornamentation of the different characters of the story. In fact, suggestive and subtle changes are the underlying key notes as emphasis is on the communication through dance itself without disturbing and distracting visions of heavy costumes. In quite a few representations, mere changes of the veil have been used as symbolic representations of the different characters.

'Muktilekha' necessitated quick changes of costume from the same set of dancers. In addition, the gamut of the saga of human rights encompassed the entire globe. Therefore, in order to deal with the challenge thus thrown up, quick changes of veils were used to jump from continent to continent or to depict different peoples in an effective and aesthetic manner.

The above representation in 'Muktilekha' was a mere adaptation of the age-old practice of the traditional Kathaks whose *gamchha* (namely a typical red-checked towel slung over the shoulder) was an all-purpose one; when getting ready for a performance, it was tied around the waist but, within seconds, it was drawn across the face as a veil typifying an extremely coy and shy heroine peeping bashfully out of her veil which in the next moment, it gave way to the brave Rajput warrior when it was tied around the head.

Kathak dance has always displayed its dynamism in its acceptance of an extension of the vocabulary of hand gestures and body movements without compromising the basic framework, character and grammar of the dance form.

Emotions, Gestures and
Movements
————— ✿ —————

When talking of dance, there is an automatic identification
of the usage of gestures and emotions with the Indian classical
dancers. Another immediate and associated identification is
that of non-comprehension of the Indian dance forms without
proper initiation into its meaning. To try and understand
this attitude, a number of basic issues come to the fore:

1. Are emotions and gestures universal or they applicable in
   the Indian context alone?
2. If they are applicable to the Indian context, how did
   they arise?
3. If they are not applicable to the Indian context alone,
   then what is the reason behind such a common
   assumption?

One of the most important aspects of dance is movement of the body communicating ideas, thoughts, feelings and desires. In the words of Aristotle in his *Poetics*, 'dance is rhythmic and whose purpose is to represent men's character as well as what they do and suffer.' In other words, besides rhythmic movements, Aristotle also stresses the expression of moods through the body. It is, therefore, not surprising when we hear that chorus groups in ancient Greece re-enacted dramatic themes during interludes which is very much akin to the Indian perception of dance. In terms of body movements throughout the world, it is seen that skipping and jumping movements are motions indicative of a happy state. Loud stamping of the feet would indicate an aggressive attitude while lowered eyes and a shrinking body attitude would indicate cowardice or shyness. Drooping of the shoulders combined with a letting-go attitude of the body would indicate sadness while a still and tense body with glazed, round eyes are universal indicators of fear. Similarly, in terms of emotions, a smile or a smiling glance are indicators of being in a happy state while a drooping, quivering mouth and lowered soulful eyes would indicate pathos and sadness. In a similar manner, the cocky attitude of a saucy gentleman or the coquettish attitude of a woman would be universally understood as would-be gestures, eye glances and body poses denoting hiding, peeping and whispering. Small cautious steps would indicate a person moving forward very carefully, without taking any risk. Similarly, trembling hands and feet combined with a bent body position would indicate old age while an unsteady walk with a swaying loosely-held body would indicate a state of drunkenness. An erect posture with the head held high would be indicative of a person of authority while a sunken chest combined with a servile attitude would be indicative of the common man. A philosopher would be represented through hunched shoulders, a deep far-away thoughtful expression and head held at an angle. A shrinking attitude and heavy breathing movement of the chest would reflect an attitude of cowardice or fear, depending on the situation.

In art, special attention is given to the representation of the character being portrayed through the body attitude. Thus, the non-verbal language indicates certain code patterns, behavioural attitudes and responses to a circumstance, with a mere glance or touch, speaking volumes. Speech may not be considered necessary at all. In other words, an action of the initiator transmits a pulse which is received by the receiver but the manner in which this pulse is received depends on the accepted universal modes of comprehension as well as the frame of mind of the receiver. The *pataka hasta* or the flat hand held horizontally above the eye-brows, palm downwards in the Indonesian dance as well as in the Japanese dance like the Indian dances are indicative of looking afar. Similarly, the right *pataka* gesture in a repeated outward throwing movement at waist level is universally understood to indicate the sowing of seeds, whether it be Indian classical or folk dances or the Indonesian, Japanese or Vietnamese folk dances from the far-eastern and south-eastern regions. The second reason has to be viewed in the context of the complexity and contradictions of human desires. Body language is the true measure of communication of ideas especially when there is a contradiction between what is said and what is meant. For example, a simple phrase like 'why have you come here?' could be expressed verbally or through body language; however, while the verbal communication may ask the question, yet if it is accompanied by a smile or a shy glance, the meaning conveyed to the receiver is just the opposite of what the words denote. In case the receiver is in a sad mood, then even a loving touch of the initiator may cause torture rather than comfort.

Another significant issue which arises is whether universality of gestures and emotions are applicable only in the context of dance or also in the context of trade and socialisation. The answer lies in all the three and it is here that we draw attention to the treatise *Theatrum Arithmetico-Geometricum* published in Leipzig in 1721. Explanatory pictorial usage of the single hand and combined hand gestures linking each gesture to certain personalities in the Bible, prophets and the Roman empire have been clearly enunciated. These were believed to have been used as a trade language. For example, the *pataka* (flat palm) denotes 'be still' while *katakamukha* opening into *alapadma* has been utilised to denote 'as wanting to speak' or 'to say something'. A *musti* (fist) denotes 'a definite attitude' and the *hamsapaksha,* 'an invitation'. The *hamsasya* pointing downwards has been utilised to indicate a miser while *sikhar* denotes acceptance. The *suchi* has been used to denote caution and two *alapadmas* put together has been used to denote a prayer while two *patakas* next to each other denote a promise.

While love in the Indian dance context is denoted by repeated opening and closing of the *mukul hasta* near the breast, the same emotion is denoted by two *sikhar hastas* placed closed to each other at the fist point.

Even with a fairly wide-ranging use of combination of hand gestures and emotions in Europe, the western classical ballet does not seemingly reflect this despite usage of such movements to a limited extent. Perhaps, one of the reasons could be due to the fact that European classical ballet is a story-telling form through a group composition with each artiste portraying a definite character, unlike most of the Indian classical dances which are examples of story-telling through the medium of a single artiste, thereby necessitating the maximum usage of gestures to denote the various characters. On the emotional front, uninhibited display of human emotions is reflected within dance enactments in India, unlike the attitude in the West where emphasis is given to curbing the tendency to give vent to emotions through facial

No:3. Hände

Nachsinnen	Überbietung	Betheuren	Treue
25	26	27	28
Freundschaft	Zornich	Nachsinnen	Weinen
29	30	31	32
Gutheißen	Loben	Weisenhintersich	Vorsich
33	34	35	36
ängstiglich	Verschwiegen	Gespöt	Einladen
37	38	39	40
Drauen	Verachten	Alto	Beschimpfen
41	42	43	44
Abschwören	Versagtheissagen	Geitzen	Sparsam
45	46	47	48

Some examples of mudras or hand gestures.

Stillen	Redenwollen	Verwundern	Vermahnen
49	50	51	52
Ängstiglich De. Kräfftigen	Negiren	aufmerck. sam machen	Ursach geben
53	54	55	56
Gewogenheit	Mitleiden	Grosmachen	Segnen
57	58	59	60
Zweiffel	Schmertz	Verstand	Willen
61	62	63	64
Gedächtnis	Wissenschaft	Mistrauen	Deut Kunst
65	66	67	68
Schwachheit	Stärcke	Beredsam. keit	Freyorth.
69	70	71	72

Some examples of mudras or hand gestures.

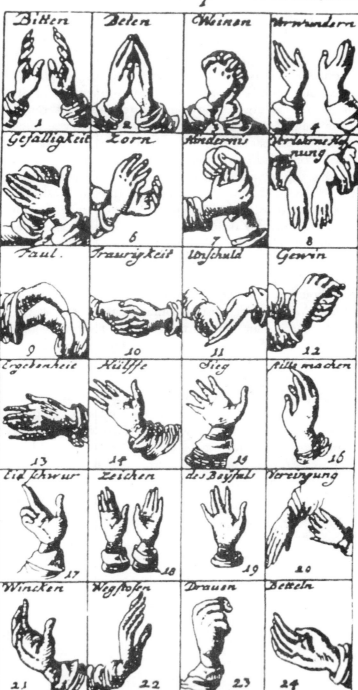

Tabula II.

No: 2 und Hände Spräch. Joh: Butwers

Some examples of mudras or hand gestures.

expressions. This has led to the emphasis on displaying emotions and moods through body movements and its tension and release. Aggression could be represented through heavy stamping of the feet in flamenco, a tense body attitude with speedy accompanying movements in western ballet and through a combination of the two in the Indian classical dance forms. Again, perhaps, it is in the area of pantomime that the usage of gestures and emotions through both the body and the face is best reflected in the West even though it is in a larger than life delineation with a touch of caricature. It differs from Indian classical dance in the sense that Indian dances eschew the element of caricature and are enactments of the story to the accompaniment of music and rhythm.

Even though the *hastas* (or hand gestures) as we know them from *Natyashastra* exist in other parts of the world, yet it is the specific meaning in the context of a culture that is important in any dance rendering. While an *alapadma* would be universally understood as a flower in full bloom a *sikharahasta* (fist with the outstretched thumb) tracing a line from the top of the left shoulder across the body to the right hip can only be understood in the Indian context as the *janeyu*, the sacred. thread worn by men of the upper castes. Similarly, representation of the flute with the requisite hand gestures would be universally understood but its allusion to Lord Krishna can only be understood in the specific Indian cultural context.

Summary

Kathak occupies an important position in the Gangetic belt encompassing within its sphere of influence, Uttar Pradesh, Rajasthan, Delhi, Bihar, parts of Gujarat, Maharashtra and Madhya Pradesh. The art of dance through story-telling was widespread in these areas. Within the temple precincts, the priests narrated divine stories which culminated in dance when these rhapsodists reached the points of ecstasy in their devotion. Hence, the dance form which originated in the temples was called 'Kathak', derived from the words 'katha' or stories and kathakars or story-tellers. This dance form was devotional and pantomimic in character, the 'katha' or story necessitating the development of a complex vocabulary of mime, gesture and 'rasa' (emotional mood and sentiment) with the passage of time.

A question which normally looms large is the date or period of its birth—whether it is of recent birth or whether, like many other dance-forms, its roots can be traced back to thousands of years. At this point of time, it may be mentioned that by looking at sculptures, literature, numismatics and such other collateral evidences, it appears that most of the Indian classical dance forms as we see them today have evolved slowly during the last 8-10 centuries. Before this, dance, per se, was prevalent as it is basic to human nature and to mankind. As far as Kathak is concerned, the earliest literary reference to Kathak is found in *Mahabharata*. The verse from the Adiparva section of *Mahabharata* mentions:

kathakascapare rajan sravanasca vanaukasah
divyakhyanani ye capi pathanti madhuram dvijah

(Arjun on his departure for the forest was accompanied amongst others by the kathaks and brahmins who recited sweetly the divine tales pleasing to the ears and eyes)

It gives succintly the profession of the kathaks while the from the *Anusasnikaparva* section mentions:

gayana nartaka cai'va vadakastartha
kathaka yodhakas cai'va rajan na rhanti ketanam

(singers, dancers, rope dancers, instrumentalists, kathaks and fighters are not to be invited for the death rites)

There are reference indicative of the kathaks belonging to the Brahmin class. These establish the fact that Kathak was well-entrenched in our system for well over 2000 years. Furthermore, an examination of the terracotta statues and figurines of dancing couples or girls and of *yakshis* (celestial door maidens) or *salabhanjikas* (celestial maidens), washed ashore by the swollen Ganges dating from the third century BC to the fifth century AD as well as the sculptures of the

Pala period covering the present day geographical area of Bihar reveal the continuity in form and stance that is adopted the Kathak dance. Historical notes on the Mauryan empire (321 BC to 187 BC) and the Guptan Empire (early fourth century to the middle of the sixth century AD), both having their capitals at Patliputra (present day Patna), and the description available in the travelogues of the Chinese travellers Fa Hien and Hiuen-Tsang are commentaries on the exalted state of music and dance. The system of guilds gave rise to hereditary professions such as the traditional kathaks.

The advent of Muslim rule in India wrought certain changes. Sculptures gave way to the painting tradition. Purdah (veil) system came into vogue and was adopted uniformly by societies of the Gangetic belt. As a result, Kathak withdrew from the populace and confined itself to the temples. During the period of Bhakti-kal, a period of religious renaissance during the 13th to the 16th century, the 'Ras-leela' tradition gained importance in the Braj area of Mathura and Vrindaban with the early 'leelas' or operatic plays being presented by Ghamand Deva and Narayan Bhatt and choreographed by the kathaks of Rajasthan. Shri Vallabha staged the 'leela' at Karhela in the 'dhrupad' style of singing with simple rhythmic patterns of Kathak which were performed by young boys before reaching puberty. This practice continues till today.

From the 17th century onwards, there was a visible resurgence of growing patronage to Kathak in the royal courts of the Hindu rulers of Darbhanga and Bettiah (in Bihar), Jaipur, Jodhpur, Udaipur and Kota in Rajasthan, Benaras in Uttar Pradesh and Raigarh and Gwalior in Madhya Pradesh, some of whom even maintained the *Guni-jan-khana* (the treasure of the virtuosos). As far as Muslim courts were concerned, it was during the reign of Nawab Wajid Ali Shah in Avadh in the 18th century that formal royal patronage was extended to a family of kathaks which had far-reaching effects. Kathak was reintroduced into active urban life and it slowly started emerging from behind the temple walls. Secondly, the 'shagirdi' (becoming a disciple) of the Nawab to a traditional Brahmin Kathak guru whose family and forefathers had danced at the temples of Hadia tehsil near Allahabad linked Kathak to the Mughal court—a fact which is often misquoted today as the origin of Kathak. Even the first census figures of James Princep in 1825 and by Buchanan in 1814 of a small area of Benaras and Bihar respectively and William Crookes in 1891 indicated the presence of an extremely large number of families of Kathak which again disproves the theory of a recent origin of the dance. The often quoted musical and dance soirees in the Court of the Delhi ruler, Muhammad Shah 'Rangile', belies the fact of an undiscriminating connoisseur of arts as his court harboured artistes of an extremely high degree of excellence and no one can call the classical singers Adarang and Sadarang, who adorned his court, mean or lesser artistes by any standard.

The 18th and 19th centuries were a prelude to the massive cultural renaissance which was to come in the 20th century. From the 19th century onwards, we see the emergence of the 'gharanas' or schools of Kathak each having its hallmark. The well-known gharanas are the Lucknow and the Jaipur followed by Benaras, Raigarh, etc.

It was the prolific system of theatre inclusive of music and dance—classical and folk—prevalent in the country which enabled the Kashmiri art historian, Bharata, to compile the *Natyashastra*. The *Natyashastra*, therefore, does not confine itself to a few dance forms but is a codification of the entire theatrics available in the country. In the codification relating to *bhramari* we find mention of the *chakra-bhramari* (spinning like a top) and the *garuda-bhramari* (spinning in a bent position).

Another characteristic feature of Kathak is the *padhant* where the dancer herself or himself recites the rhythmic *bols* or syllables before dancing, which is a hangover and a continuing tradition of the kathaks of the temples in ancient Hindu India where enactment was preceded by recitation.

A usual Kathak performance will start with a *stuti* or a *vandana* (prayer to the Lord) followed by introduction of rhythmic patterns from the simplistic to the complicated. These are followed by various *abhinaya* or mime sequences. Mention must be made of the *gat-bhava* where a whole story comprising of more than one character is enacted to the accompaniment of rhythm but with no supportive text, highlighting thereby the usage of *mudras* (symbolic hand gestures), *hastas* (hand gestures) and *rasas* (emotional sentiments and moods). In addition, the repertoire consists of many items: the *thumri* (verses which highlight the romantic element and are usually based on Radha and Krishna as the principal characters), *dhrupad, dhamar, ghazal* (Urdu poetry), *bhajan* (devotional songs), *chaturang* (a rhythmic musical piece having four sections each with its distinctive character), *kavitt* and *prahelika-kavitt*, etc. where *abhinaya* is enacted to a text. *Dhrupad* compositions are rich, dignified, sombre in carriage and architecture while *dhamar* compositions, usually set to a cycle of fourteen beats and sung on the occasion of *Holi* (the colour festival of the Hindus marking the end of winter and the onset of summer), are more sprightly in character.

A Kathak performance would usually end with a *tarana* (rhythmical, lyrical compositions where the mnemonics used are meaningless, symbolising the need for no words at the height of ecstasy of spiritual union) and rhythmic patterns done to very fast tempo and a range of footwork. The movements and *abhinaya* employed within Kathak are life-like and natural with no unnatural exaggeration. The element of *upaj* or *improvisation* both in the rhythmic field as well as in *abhinaya* is perhaps the strongest in Kathak. *Upaj* in *abhinaya* is best demonstrated in the *bhav batana* where each line or each word is interpreted in a myriad ways. *Upaj*, therefore, is the hallmark of any senior well-known Kathak artiste. Besides the traditional repertoire, new innovations including dance-dramas and enactment of philosophical, abstract and modern themes have been most prolific in Kathak.

The accompaniment to Kathak is provided by *tabla* (two piece drum), *pakhawaj* (a large horizontal drum, traditionally called *mridanga*), vocalist, sitar (a fretted, plucked *string* instrument), flute, etc. The music is based on the North Indian Classical Music system.

The costume of the Kathak is not far removed from life itself and reflects the costume of the people. The costumes of the male Kathak range from the traditional *dhoti-bandi* to the *churidar-angarkha* and for the women from the *lehenga-choli* to the *churidar-angarkha*. (Dhoti is a traditional cloth wrapped around the waist with its ends tucked between the legs; *bandi* is a kind of shirt while *churidar* is a tight fitting trouser; *angarkha* is a kind of top which takes the form of a long frock where the lady dancer is concerned, *lehenga* is an ankle-length skirt while *choli* is a blouse).

The second half of the 20th century has seen many old traditions which though adopted in the last 400-500 years have now been broken as more and more girls from well-to-do, respectable families are taking to dance as a form of art, with quite a few amongst them aspiring to become full-fledged professionals.

REGIONS COVERED IN THE *NATYASHASTRA*

References to the following places have been made in Chapters XIV, XVIII and XXIII of the *Natyashastra* (in alphabetical order) covering the entire Indian subcontinent:

Location in *Natyashastra*	Present day location
• Anarta	North-west Gujarat
• Anga	North Bihar
• Antargiri	Upper Himalayan belt
• Andhra	Deccan, Andhra Pradesh
• Arvuda	Abu, Rajasthan
• Avarta	Gangetic plain
• Avanti	Ujjain, Madhya Pradesh
• Bahirgiri	Tibet
• Bhargava	Kathiawar region, Gujarat
• Brahmottara	Bay of Bengal
• Carmanvati	Chambal, northern Madhya Pradesh
• Daksingiri	Sanchi, MP
• Daksinamal	Gorakhpur, UP
• Daksinapath	south of Vindhyachal
• Dramida	Tamil Nadu
• Ganga	Gangetic belt
• Himalaya	Himalayan region
• Kasmira	Kashmir
• Kalanga	district Dehradun, Uttar Pradesh
• Kalinga	south Orissa
• Kulinga	region between Sutlej and Beas, Punjab
• Kosala	Ayodhya, Uttar Pradesh
• Khasa	Kumaon region, Uttar Pradesh
• Magadh	Central and southern Bihar

• Malava	Malwa, Madhya Pradesh
• Maharastra	Maharashtra
• Mahendra	Eastern Ghats
• Malaya	Nilgiri region, Karnataka
• Martikavatak	district Alwar, Rajasthan
• Masalli	district Kolar, Mysore
• Mekala	Vindhyachal
• Nepal	Nepal
• Odra or Udra	Orissa
• Pancala	region around Bareilly, Badaun and Farukkhabad
• Paundra	Deccan plateau
• Pragjyotisa	Gauhati, Assam
• Pulindabhumi	Tibet
• Saulaka	district Campbellpur, Pakistan
• Salava	Alwar, Rajasthan
• Sauvira	southern Sindh in Pakistan, Gujarat and southern Punjab
• Sahya	Western Ghats
• Sindhu	Indus belt of Pakistan and Punjab
• Suhmottara	Bay of Bengal
• Saurasena	Mathura, Uttar Pradesh
• Surastra	Saurashtra, Gujarat
• Tamralipta	district Mednipur, West Bengal
• Tosala	Orissa
• Tripura	Tripura, North-eastern India
• Videha	Mithila region
• Vatsa	southern Allahabad
• Vanavasa	northern Karnataka
• Vahlika	Punjab
• Vidisa	Vidisha, Madhya Pradesh
• Vetravati	Betwa region near Malwa, MP.

(The identification of these places have been taken from the compilation, *Aitihasik Sthanavali*, by Vijayendra Kumar Mathur, published by the Ministry of Education, Government of India, in 1969. The present day locations of Pramsu-pravritti, Plavamga, Kalapanjara and Margava could not be identified. However, there are references to Kalijara and Mrigadav identified as district Banda in Uttar Pradesh and Sarnath respectively.)

Select Readings

1) *Natya Shastra*
2) *Monograph on Bharata's Natyashastra* by P.S.R. Appa Rao
3) *Abhinaya Darpan*
4) *Mirror of Gestures* by Ananda Coomaraswamy
5) *Mahabharata*
6) *Ramayana*
7) *Classical Indian Dances in Literature and the Arts* by Kapila Vatsyayan
8) *Indian Classical Dance* by Kapila Vatsyayan
9) *The Dance in India* by Enakshi Bhavnani
10) *Kathak Nritya* by L.N. Garg
11) *Kathak* by P. Banerji
12) Kathak by Dr. Sunil Kothari
13) *An Introduction to Indian Music* by B. Chaitanya Deva
14) *Tal Ank* by R.L. Garg
15) *The Miracle Plays of Mathura* by Norvin Hein

16) *Kathak Nritya Shiksha* by Dr. Puru Dadheech
17) *Sangeet Makarand* by Shree Narad
18) *The Evolution of Khayal* by M.V. Dhond
19) *A History of India* by Romila Thapar
20) *Bhartya Vidya Bhawan Series on Indian History*
21) *Indien in Wort und Bild* by Schlagintweit
22) *Aitihasik Sthanavali* by V.K. Mathur
23) *Brahma Mahapurana*
24) *Ain-e-akbari*
25) *Sangeet Damodara*
26) *Hindi Sahitya Ka Itihas* by Ramchandra Shukla
27) *Reeti Kaleen Ke Kaviyan*
28) *Persian Art* by S. Maslenitsyana
29) *Qajar Paintings* by S.J. Falk
30) *Persian Women and their Ways* by Clara Rice
31) *Indian Archaeology* by V.S. Agarwal
32) *History of Fine Arts in India and Ceylon* by Smith
33) *Notes on Early Indian Art* by Dr. Radha Kumud Mookerji
34) *Buddhist Monks and Monasteries of India* by Sukumar Dutta
35) *The Art and Architecture of India* by Benjamin Rowland
36) *Sangeet Ratnakar* by Sharangadeva
37) *Theatrum Arithmetico Geometricum* by Christoph Buntel
38) *Seminar papers on Kathak*
39) *Manu Smriti*
40) *Vikramorvasiya* by Kalidasa
41) *Catalogues of Allahabad Museum*
42) *Catalogues of Mathura Museum*
43) *Catalogues of Patna Museum*
44) *The Dance of Siva* by Coomaraswamy
45) *Indian Architecture* by E.B. Havell
46) *The Hindu temples* by Stella Kramnisch
47) *Rajput Painting* by Coomaraswamy
48) *A Short Historical Survey of Music of Upper India* by Bhatkhande

49) *Catalogue from the exhibition on Egypt at Linz*
50) *The Art and Architecture of the Indian Subcontinent* by J.C. Harle
51) *The Position of Women in Hindu civilization* by A.S. Altekar
52) *Dastan-e-Patliputra* by Ramji Mishra 'Manohar'
53) *Bihar: Ek Sanskritik Gaurav* (compiled by Dr. Shankar Dayal Singh)
54) *Jataka Stories*
55) *Therigatha*
56) *Lalitvistara*
57) *Mahavastu*
58) *Deeghnikaya*
59) *Vinaypitaka*
60) *SriHastamuktavali* by Shubhankar
61) *Banni* by N. Wajid Ali Shah
62) *Courtesans* by Motichand
63) *Bharatiya Veshabhoosha* by Motichand
64) *Mathura ki Butkala* by Agrawal
65) *Buchanan's Survey of Bihar*
66) *Yagnavalkyasmriti*
67) *Meghdoot by* Kalidasa
68) *Vidyapati Padavali*
69) *The Tantric Way* by Mukherji and Khanna

Appendix

Genealogical tree of Lucknow Gharana

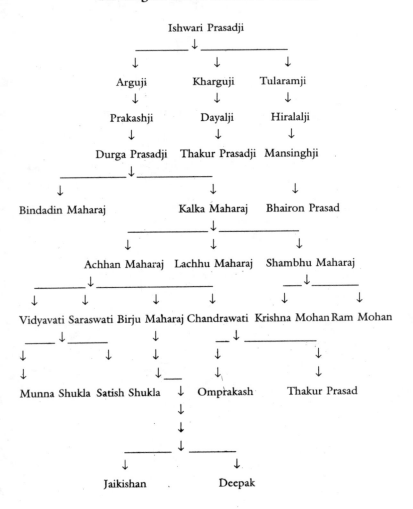

Geneological trees of Jaipur Gharana

<u>Table 1</u>

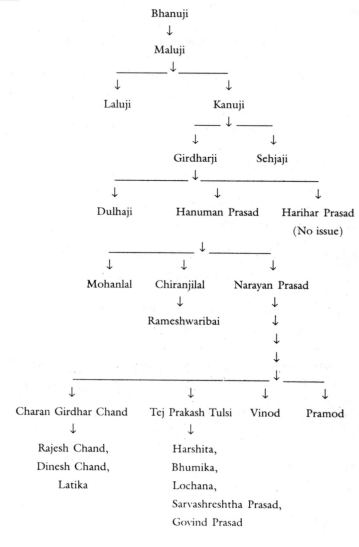

Table 2

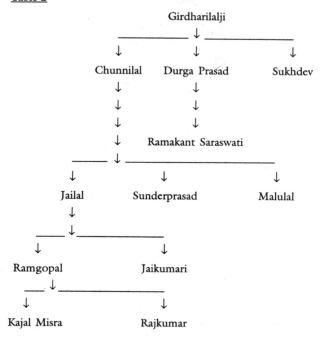

Table 3

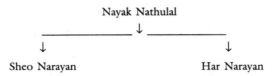

Nayak Nathulal

Sheo Narayan   Har Narayan

<u>Table 4</u>

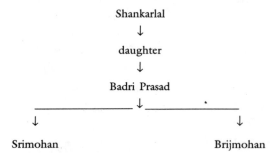

Shankarlal
↓
daughter
↓
Badri Prasad

↓   ↓

Srimohan   Brijmohan

Table 5

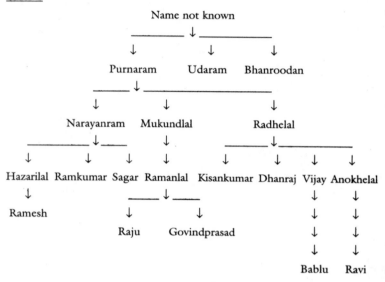

Table 6

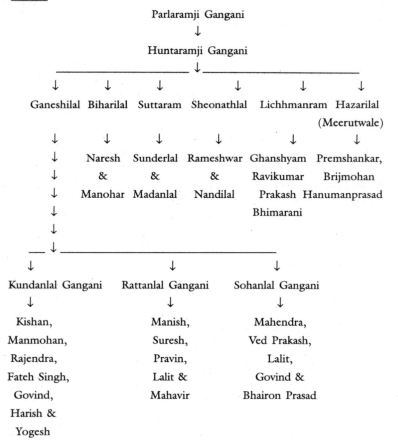

Genelogical trees of Janki Prasad Gharana
(or Benaras Gharana I)

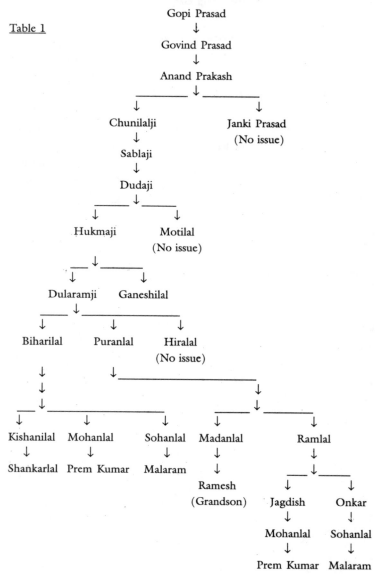

Table 1

Gopi Prasad
↓
Govind Prasad
↓
Anand Prakash
├─────────────┬─────────────┤
Chunilalji   Janki Prasad
↓   (No issue)
Sablaji
↓
Dudaji
├──────┬──────┤
Hukmaji   Motilal
(No issue)

Dularamji   Ganeshilal

Biharilal   Puranlal   Hiralal
(No issue)

Kishanilal   Mohanlal   Sohanlal   Madanlal   Ramlal
↓   ↓   ↓   ↓   ↓
Shankarlal   Prem Kumar Malaram   ↓
                                    Ramesh   Jagdish   Onkar
                                    (Grandson) ↓   ↓
                                                Mohanlal   Sohanlal
                                                ↓   ↓
                                                Prem Kumar Malaram

Table 2

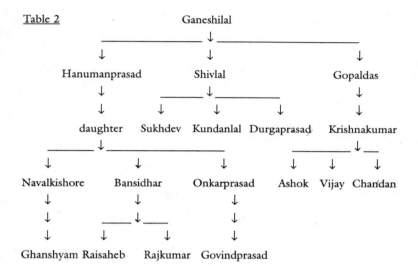

Geneological tree of the Benaras Gharana II

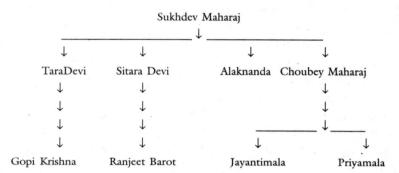

Sukhdev Maharaj

TaraDevi   Sitara Devi   Alaknanda Choubey Maharaj

Gopi Krishna   Ranjeet Barot   Jayantimala   Priyamala